W9-DFP-813

KILLER
GIRLFRIEND

KILLER
GIRLFRIEND

THE JODI ARIAS STORY

BRIAN SKOLOFF & JOSH HOFFNER

BEAUFORT
BOOKS

Copyright © 2013 by Brian Skoloff and Josh Hoffner

First Edition

All rights reserved. No part of this book may be reproduced in any form or by any electronic or mechanical means, including information storage and retrieval systems, without permission in writing from the publisher, except by a reviewer who may quote brief passages in a review.

Library of Congress Cataloging-in-Publication Data Available

ISBN: 978-0-8253-0727-0

For inquiries about volume orders, please contact:

Beaufort Books
27 West 20th Street, Suite 1102
New York, NY 10011
sales@beaufortbooks.com

Published in the United States by Beaufort Books
www.beaufortbooks.com

Distributed by Midpoint Trade Books
www.midpointtrade.com

Printed in the United States of America
Interior design by Elyse Strongin, Neuwirth & Associates, Inc.
Cover Design by Michael Williams

R0428638986

CONTENTS

ACKNOWLEDGEMENTS

This book came together in short order, and we believe it provides a gripping and comprehensive account of the entire Jodi Arias and Travis Alexander saga. We hoped to not only provide readers with a full account of the case, from the killing to the verdict, but to delve deeper into the lives of both Jodi and Travis before they met each other and embarked on a tragic journey.

We'd like to thank our editors, Katie Oyan and Anna Jo Bratton, for their tireless efforts aimed at making sure the book offered a true and factual account of the case, and did so in a way that flowed from start to finish.

We'd also like to thank San Francisco-area criminal defense attorney Michael Cardoza for his never-ending encouragement throughout this project and Los Angeles-area criminal defense lawyer Mark Geragos for providing insightful offerings on the legal system. Phoenix criminal defense lawyer Julio Laboy also contributed a great deal of insight for the book.

Wild About Trial founder Alison Triessl wrote the foreword that put this book into the context of the social media environment that helped make the case such a national sensation, and Wild About Trial reporter and digital artist Michael

Williams contributed incredible work on the book's cover and website.

We offer a big thanks to Waterfront Digital Press and Vook, along with our agent, Bill Gladstone and publisher Jack Jennings, for their constant support and encouragement.

And lastly, we'd like to thank our managers at *The Associated Press* for affording us the opportunity to pursue this project, and the entire company for giving us a platform to tell this story and so many others over the years.

—BRIAN SKOLOFF and JOSH HOFFNER

FOREWORD

This country has watched its share of mesmerizing criminal trials over the past 20 years.

Much of the media attention began with O.J. Simpson and his ensuing case dubbed the "Trial of the Century."

The immense public interest only continued with the likes of Scott Peterson, Conrad Murray, Robert Blake, Phil Spector, Casey Anthony, Drew Peterson and a handful of others.

But nobody could have foreseen the impact that an unknown Northern California waitress would have on changing the media's approach to following criminal trials. This book is the story of Jodi Arias and the trial that captivated a nation as it became a cable TV news sensation and lit up the world of social media like no other before.

Over the past year, my company, Wild About Trial, has scoured the country looking for the most interesting criminal trials, often relying on the steady stream of content from The Associated Press in populating our site.

We are a website and mobile app designed to provide live streaming of trials accompanied by a complete interactive experience including live tweeting from inside the courtroom, legal analysis from our staff of attorneys, official court documents, and community forums.

From day one of the Jodi Arias trial and continuing on through the verdict, we saw a dynamic shift in how viewers consumed every facet of the case.

In this modern era of instantaneous news, the public demanded up-to-the-second updates on every element of the trial. They read stories from the AP and other news organizations, but they also wanted to watch it live, in real time, and wanted to peek behind the curtain. So they went to the only logical place today's public goes to find immediate information: Twitter.

An entire interactive community developed around the Jodi Arias trial.

Wild About Trial placed a reporter in the courtroom live tweeting every update on the case and answering viewer questions, providing the site's followers with the next best thing to being inside the courtroom itself.

As the online conversation developed, many viewers began to feel left behind if they missed even a single day. The Jodi Arias trial became much more than water cooler talk. It became a must-watch event—and people were watching it everywhere, on their home or work computers and even on their mobile devices so they never had to miss a moment.

The authors of this book are veteran Associated Press journalists who have each spent more than a decade covering the nation's most newsworthy stories from the 9-11 terrorist attacks to Hurricane Katrina, the Fort Hood shootings, the Gulf of Mexico oil spill, the Colorado movie theater massacre and the Scott Peterson murder trial, just to name a few. They are able to bring this wealth of experience into their narrative to provide a complete account of the facts in this sensational trial, as well as provide a greater context to understand why the story of a small-town woman accused of murder captivated so many.

This book provides the first comprehensive account of the case from the day Jodi and Travis Alexander met to the killing, Jodi's arrest, her ensuing trial and finally, the verdict, written by a journalist who sat in the courtroom throughout every twist and turn of the four-month trial, along with his veteran AP editor. It is a gripping page-turner that covers the entirety of the Jodi Arias saga, perfect for the most avid Jodi Arias trial-watcher or even those just trying to find out what all the fuss is about.

—ALISON TRIESSL
Wild About Trial, Founder;
co-founder and CEO of the Pasadena Recovery Center;
Attorney

1

THE KILLING

"Heaven has no rage like love to hatred turned,
Nor hell a fury like a woman scorned."

—William Congreve

Travis couldn't help himself. Jodi was every man's dream. The sex was fantastic. She was up for anything, you name it. The petite, brown-haired—sometimes blond—seductive 27-year-old was a pleaser, willing to satisfy Travis' every kinky desire.

On this day in June 2008, the 30-year-old Travis was ready for more. He was preparing to head off on a trip to Cancun with a devoutly Mormon woman who made it crystal clear she wasn't interested in anything beyond a platonic relationship.

But Travis had Jodi. And despite wanting to marry a good woman of faith, he had carnal desires that deeply conflicted with the man he presented himself to be publicly.

Jodi served a purpose. She was never Mrs. Right, just Miss Right Now as Travis fulfilled his sexual needs before hopefully meeting The One.

This never sat well with Jodi.

She arrived at about 4 a.m. from California during what was supposed to be a road trip to see another man in Utah. Arizona was hundreds of miles off her course, but she couldn't resist Travis' charm and her overwhelming desire to please him. She was blinded by her love for the handsome, confident and outgoing professional who gave rousing motivational speeches to cheering colleagues at conferences across the country. His smile lit up the room and melted her heart. It was never clear whether Travis had invited Jodi to come to see him that day. Authorities contend he had not, but Jodi insisted he begged her to visit.

The two crawled into his king-size bed together. When they awoke in the afternoon at about 1 p.m. in Travis's tidy four-bedroom home in Mesa outside Phoenix, the day began like so many others with the pair, naked and sexual.

But according to police, that's not all Jodi had in mind. She came for revenge. She came to teach Travis a lesson. She came to kill.

Less than five hours later, Travis would be dead.

Exactly what happened during those remaining hours of Travis' life is known only by two people—Travis and Jodi—and Jodi is the only one still alive to fill in the gaps.

According to Jodi, the day began with steamy sex and eventually devolved into a harrowing fight for her life.

Her rendition of the final hours of Travis' life—and what came after—follows:

Travis always wanted to tie her to the bed for a raunchy romp, so she complied. He loosely tied her wrists to his headboard before the sex began.

Travis later had other plans—for the two to take nude photos of each other, yet another deviant fantasy he privately harbored. Jodi naked in pigtails on the bed, splayed out on his mattress. Graphic, pornographic, close-up photos of Jodi's genitalia. A photo of Travis lying naked on his back.

Just a few hours later, Travis wanted her to take photographs of him in the shower, proud of his newly fit body after months of working out ahead of the trip to Mexico.

One photo of Travis in the shower was taken at about 5:30 that evening. Another was taken a short time later, a chilling tight shot of Travis' face, water beads dripping from his cheeks, his eyes focused in a serious gaze.

Jodi then accidentally dropped his new camera, sending him into a rage. He lunged in anger, body slamming her to the tile floor. She managed to escape his firm grasp and wriggled free.

Travis chased her from the bathroom in a fury. She ran into his closet to retrieve a .25-caliber pistol he kept on a shelf, then fled out another door at the opposite end in a dash for the hallway—with Travis still in pursuit and clearly enraged.

He lunged at her again. She fired the gun, but didn't know if the bullet struck him. He just kept coming. And now Jodi's memory failed her. Her mind grew foggy, the trauma of the attack washing her brain of any recollection of what happened next.

She conceded she must have stabbed him numerous times, but can't recall where she got the knife, or anything after that until she finds herself about 280 miles north near the Hoover Dam in Nevada, pulled onto the side of the road, her hands drenched in blood. She knew something terrible had happened, but just couldn't remember the details.

"I must have killed him," she thought to herself. Stricken with fear and shame, Jodi ditched the gun somewhere in the desert—she has no idea what she did with the knife—and headed north to Salt Lake City to see the other man. But not before starting a chain of events aimed at meticulously creating an alibi to avoid suspicion.

She would later claim she was never at Travis' house that day. She sent him text messages and emails within hours of killing him, and left him a message on his mobile phone apologizing for not being able to make it for a visit as he had wanted.

Jodi then continued north to Salt Lake City where she met the man she had originally planned to meet and spent the night in his bed kissing and cuddling as if nothing had happened. As if she hadn't just washed Travis' blood from her hands. As if Travis was still alive and not crumpled dead in his shower with nearly 30 stab wounds, his throat slit from ear to ear so deeply she nearly cut his head clean off, a bullet hole in his forehead.

She would go on with her life, returning to Northern California for her regular waitressing shifts, and her normal routine for roughly the next month until her arrest.

Then came the lies.

First, she wasn't there.

Next, masked intruders carried out the attack and she escaped.

Two years after Jodi was jailed on a first-degree murder charge, and faced with irrefutable evidence of her involvement in the killing, the self-defense story emerged. And to this day, she is sticking to that story.

Police present a much more chilling scenario of Travis' death, one of blind rage and vengeance, an attack so ferocious it's hard to imagine that the soft-spoken librarian-like woman later seen in the courtroom could have been behind it.

Authorities say Jodi snapped, tired of being used by Travis for sex while he courted other women he had hoped would be the marrying type.

Travis didn't even know Jodi was coming, let alone that she would be arriving armed with a .25 caliber pistol she took from her grandparents, making sure he would never get the chance to fulfill his dreams of becoming a family man and settling down with another woman.

After the day of sex, Travis took a shower. Jodi begged him to let her take photos while he washed off. He caved, begrudgingly.

Then something set her off. Something he said. Something he did. The way he looked at her with disgust. She was reminded of the times he called her a whore and a skank, when he said she was nothing more to him than a "three-hole wonder." And of the trip he planned to take to Mexico with another woman. He never invited Jodi. This enraged her.

At some point, Travis' guard was down, he was comfortable, not expecting the murderous rage that was about to be unleashed on him. Jodi was about to carry out her plan.

She pulled out a knife and suddenly began stabbing him in the chest. Travis was stunned. He struggled to grab the blade. It sliced through the tender skin of his palms. He stumbled in a daze around the bathroom, at one point hunching over the sink, where blood spilled out everywhere.

Jodi stabbed him again and again, in the chest, in the back, in the head. He struggled to speak, gasping and gurgling, in shock by the blitz attack and the sheer pain of the deep gashes all over his body.

He began to lose strength as he bled profusely. Jodi then

went in for the kill, and with a powerful slashing motion cut his throat wide open. Blood was now spewing from his neck.

The medical examiner would later conclude this knife wound was likely fatal, as Travis would have quickly bled to death, both his carotid arteries that deliver blood from the heart to the brain severed.

But Jodi wasn't done. At some point, she pulled out the gun and polished Travis off with a single shot to the forehead. Authorities would later claim he was already dead at that point, and the gunshot was just one final salvo of rage. Jodi dragged his mutilated body back into his shower, and washed off much of the blood.

She then began to clean the scene, but left blood everywhere along with her hair and bloody palm print. She deleted the nude photos, and put the camera in Travis' washing machine then turned it on, for whatever reason leaving behind evidence of her involvement.

Later, she simply grabbed her things, walked out the front door to her car, and drove off as if nothing had happened.

2

JODI AND TRAVIS

"I will find an eternal companion that enhances me exponentially and countless other goals that at one point I dare not even dream."

—Travis Alexander

By now, the world is familiar with Jodi Arias. She went on trial for Travis' death in January, 2013 and her story has provided an endless fascination to people around the world.

The image of a bespectacled Arias sitting in a Phoenix courtroom—often crying and wearing drab outfits—became a daily fixture in the news for more than four months.

The story of Travis and Jodi is one of troubled upbringings, passion, love, betrayal, the Mormon church, and most notably, sex, something that would remain a constant theme throughout her trial.

Jodi Ann Arias was born on July 9, 1980, in Salinas, California, a city best known as the hometown of John Steinbeck, and often referred to as the "salad bowl of the world" because it is such a prolific agricultural region.

Her parents are Bill and Sandy Arias.

Bill owned restaurants all through Jodi's childhood—and still does to this day. Sandy also worked in the family restaurant until she became a dental assistant in the early 1990s. Jodi joined the business herself as a teenager, waiting tables after school and on weekends.

Jodi was the oldest of four siblings, including brothers Carl and Joseph and sister Angela. She was closest to Carl in age, and she fondly recalls an idyllic early childhood with him that involved bike-riding, tree-climbing, camping, roller-skating, and playing with friends in their cul-de-sac in Salinas. She played the flute, enjoyed art, and took karate lessons.

The family left Salinas when she was about 11 and moved to Santa Maria, about an hour north of Santa Barbara, where Jodi spent her junior high years. The family eventually settled in the former gold rush town of Yreka, located in far Northern California near the Oregon border.

She attended Yreka Union High School for three years, with Spanish and art being her favorite classes. She liked Spanish so much that she took a study abroad trip to Costa Rica.

The relationship between Jodi and her parents was strained. She'd act up and get scolded like many adolescents. In 8th grade, her parents caught her growing marijuana at the house. They called the cops, and Jodi always resented them for it.

Jodi claimed during her trial that her parents were abusive, giving her spankings with various objects, including a wooden spoon and belt, and shoving her into furniture, a door post and a piano in punishments that allegedly grew worse as she got older.

She says her dad was a physically imposing man, claiming that he could once bench press an astounding 520 pounds. However, her abuse claims were not corroborated by anyone else, and it doesn't appear any of it was ever reported to authorities. Jodi's parents were never called to testify during the guilt phase of the trial and largely declined to comment throughout the proceedings.

The relationship with her parents grew more tumultuous as time went on.

The tipping point came when Jodi got caught skipping school at the end of her junior year, and her parents grounded her until her 18th birthday. It was to be a rigid grounding—no phone, no contact with friends, essentially confinement to her room until July.

In the weeks prior, Jodi had already been plotting her escape as she fought more with her parents, quietly packing up and moving boxes to the home of an older guy she had fallen in love with. When the grounding came, Jodi moved out and later dropped out of high school. She got her GED in jail.

Jodi loved art from a young age. She was always drawing and painting pictures. Although she is often referred to in the media as an aspiring photographer, Jodi never really took those aspirations very far, other than a few wedding gigs. She loved shooting photos, yes, she shot thousands and thousands of them, but Jodi's real profession was as a waitress.

She worked at least 10 different restaurant jobs in the decade or so from her teenage years until she was arrested at the age of 28. The locations ran the gamut from a high-end luxury hotel to a Denny's to a California Pizza Kitchen located in a mall. She tended bar, waited tables and became quite good at it, in fact.

Jodi's big foray into the professional world was at a company called Prepaid Legal Services.

Prepaid Legal was founded in the 1970s by an Oklahoma businessman named Harland Stonecipher, who had trouble paying his legal bills after a bad car accident.

He founded a company that allowed members to pay a monthly fee to get access to legal and other services. The company is now called Legal Shield, and it offers identity theft protection as one of its main services.

The company made Stonecipher a multimillionaire—and enticed thousands of other Americans with the same tantalizing prospect.

Prepaid Legal is similar to Amway in that it relies on an aggressive sales force to spread the message and recruit new salespeople to get rewarded financially.

Jodi met Travis at a Prepaid Legal conference. Her life pretty much spiraled from that point forward.

Jodi's childhood seemed downright idyllic when compared to Travis' upbringing. His mother was an addict, hooked on methamphetamine just as the drug was becoming the scourge of communities all across America.

As a result, Travis and his siblings were subjected to all sorts of ills that no child should ever have to encounter. His father was addicted to drugs, too, but got clean before he died. Travis was always proud of his dad for turning his life around.

Travis described in his blog how awful it was in their neighborhood in Riverside, California. Mom would be strung out for days, then she would come home and need to crash for several more days. Travis would attempt to wake her up, and he'd get beaten. "It hurt, but we got used to it," he wrote.

They also got used to not having much food around the house. Meth took priority over groceries, so Travis and his siblings would have to literally scrounge for crumbs.

He remembers one day from his childhood when all he could find in the house to eat was a moldy piece of bread. The house was disgustingly filthy, too—so much so that roaches infested the family's surroundings.

The cops showed up on a regular basis amid a series of domestic disturbances between his mother and father, including a time when mom emptied a handgun into dad's car and another occasion where dad took an ax to mom's belongings.

"I have never heard in any movie, on any street corner, or amongst the vilest of men any string of words so offensive and hateful, said with such disgust as was the words that my mother said to my sisters and I," Travis wrote in his blog.

The family eventually got kicked out of the house, requiring them to move into a camper in his aunt's backyard—leaving them crammed into the tiny space for about a year. Travis didn't bathe much, and naturally got mocked at school for his filthy appearance.

The camper was right next to a washing machine. The discharge wasn't connected to any sewer system, so it dumped piles of wastewater right next to their ramshackle temporary home.

Finally, Travis and his siblings got the hell out of there. They moved in with his grandmother when Travis was about 10 and never looked back. He had seven siblings in all; both his parents are now deceased.

Grandmother Norma Sarvey took Travis under her wing, taught him how to be a man, and introduced him to the Mormon faith. During the screaming matches with his mother, Travis had prayed and come to believe that God was somehow looking out for him—if he could just get out of this mess.

He was naturally drawn to religion after all he went through.

Travis was baptized into the Mormon church, did a two-year mission in Denver, and eventually became a fun-loving, successful salesman and motivational speaker at Prepaid Legal.

In the early 2000s he moved to Mesa—a perfect spot for a young Mormon man. The city is home to one of the largest Mormon populations in the country outside Utah.

He became a fitness nut, obsessively counting calories and working out. He loved the sport of Mixed Martial Arts and was a big believer in environmentally friendly causes in the months before he died, buying a hybrid electric Toyota Prius.

Colleagues at Prepaid Legal would cheer loudly when he walked to the stage at seminars, conferences, and team meetings, encouraging them to sell, sell, sell. Only 5-foot-9 in height, he became a larger-than-life figure to some colleagues. His message was refreshing, his approach authentic. He once showed up with a 1980s heavy metal-style wig and a muscle shirt at a Prepaid Legal conference, leading a skit as a character named Eddie Snell from Alabama. As a Def Leppard tune blared, he danced around the front of the room and had the crowd on their feet, absolutely loving every bit of it. He was completely comfortable cutting it up onstage.

The adversity of his youth shaped his adulthood and helped make him an optimist in every sense of the word. When life throws something bad your way, it's not a stumbling block, he would say, it's a stepping-stone!

In a poignant blog post in early 2008, Travis outlined his big dreams and visions for the year ahead. It was vintage Travis: enthusiasm, confidence, ready to take on the world and make it a better place.

This Year will be the Best year of my life. This is the year that will eclipse all others. I will earn more, learn more, travel more, serve more, love more, give more and be more than all the other years of my life combined. True other years now past have been at times magnificent but none like this. This is a year of metamorphosis, of growth and accomplishment that at previous was unimaginable.

He circled back to the "best year of his life" mantra in the final sentence of the blog post, right after offering this prediction: "I will find an eternal companion that enhances me exponentially and countless other goals that at one point I dare not even dream."

A few months later, he was dead.

3

THE LOVES OF JODI'S LIFE

*"She's come undone. She wanted truth but all she got was lies.
Came the time to realize, and it was too late."*

—The Guess Who

Jodi had three loves in her life before she met Travis: Bobby
Juarez, Matt McCartney, and Darryl Brewer. Only Darryl
would be called to testify at her trial.

The relationships were all unusual and tormented in their
own ways.

She met Bobby Juarez at a carnival as a teenager. She was
standing next to a ride called the Zipper when she noticed him,
seduced by his long black hair and goth attire that stood out
on a sweltering summer day.

The Zipper is a fast ride in which occupants get strapped
into a cage that spins around in circles as it hurtles through the
air. That stomach-churning, terrifying, unpredictable ride was
the beginning of Jodi's turbulent romantic life.

At the time, she was an impressionable 15-year-old, and
Bobby was a skinny 18-year-old with no job, who had all sorts

of wild ideas and beliefs. He believed in vampires and wanted to travel to San Francisco to hunt them, an idea that intrigued Jodi, who was a big fan of Anne Rice books at the time. But the relationship was not without problems. At one point Bobby tried to strangle her, according to Jodi, and told her "how he would kill each member of my family."

Jodi says she tried calling 911 during one fight, but Bobby snatched the phone from her hand and hung up. The 911 operator called back, but Bobby made up an excuse that his girlfriend was trying to program 911 into the speed dial and it was an accident.

She ended the relationship with her young love, and said she later learned he was so distraught that he had slit his wrists to attempt suicide. Jodi later reconnected with him after a man she met at her father's restaurant told her that the second coming of Jesus Christ would happen sometime in late 1997.

She rushed to warn Bobby about the impending Rapture.

She soon fell in love again—this time with Matt McCartney, Bobby's one-time roommate.

Matt was living in Medford, Oregon, just up the freeway from Yreka, and as the flame died out between her and Bobby, she now had a new love interest.

Jodi got a job at an Applebee's, and she and Matt later worked in the service industry in the picturesque Crater Lake National Park area, a popular spot for tourists and skiers. They lived together for a while and got in minor fights over things like dirty dishes and messes left around the house.

The small fights eventually led them to take a breather from living together, and she took a job in nearby Ashland while he stayed on at Crater Lake.

Jodi said the relationship ended after she caught him cheating with a Romanian co-worker named Bianca. After hearing about the rumored affair, Jodi left early from her restaurant shift and drove the hour and a half from Ashland to Crater Lake to confront Bianca.

A friend let her into the dormitories where seasonal workers stay. She and Bianca sat on the two beds in the room and talked about it, in what Jodi described as a long, tearful chat. She then tracked down Matt, confronted him about the affair, and the relationship was over.

This version of events is Jodi's alone. Matt has not spoken publicly about their relationship. But even in her version of events, she was willing to make the drive to physically confront a woman she suspected of cheating with her lover. Her obsessive nature was already becoming obvious.

Jodi then found out about a sweet gig at an elite boutique resort in Big Sur, California, called the Ventana Inn and Spa.

The Ventana Inn—tucked away off the famed Pacific Coast Highway amid lush tree-covered hills and dramatic cliffs dropping into the deep blue ocean—can safely be described as one of the most picturesque hotels in America, and it doesn't come cheap. Rooms routinely exceed $600 a night.

She began working there in the fall of 2001. It was at Ventana that she met Darryl Brewer.

At the time, Jodi was 21 and Darryl was 41 and recently divorced. Not only was he 20 years her senior, he was her boss. He had a young son who was closer in age to Jodi than she was to Darryl.

Still, she developed a crush on him. She didn't mind the thought of dating an older man whom she saw as a George Clooney-type with his salt-and-pepper hair. They became closer the longer they worked together, as Jodi waited the tables of wealthy guests and later transferred to wedding planning and coordination in the summer of 2002. The wedding gig was an exciting one for Jodi as she got to immerse herself in the inner-workings of planning the biggest night of couples' lives. Time and again, she saw people who had found their own eternal loves. Jodi wanted that more than anything.

Darryl left his position as food and beverage manager and became a member of the wait staff. Finally, he was no longer her boss. The relationship was on.

The pair traveled to the Bay Area where they went on sight-seeing trips and attended football games to see their favorite team—the San Francisco 49ers. Jodi is a big 49ers fan, and they had fun seeing Terrell Owens and their other favorite players in action. They talked about their future together, with Darryl warning that he wasn't interested in marriage.

The two fell in love.

The sex was good, too. They experimented with anal sex—another oddity that would emerge again and again throughout Jodi's murder trial.

Always the amateur photographer, Jodi took provocative pictures of Darryl in the nude and in the shower. She took pictures of Darryl shaving, when he slept, on all sorts of other occasions. She liked to take pictures of Travis, too.

Jodi eventually left Ventana and went to work as a waitress and bartender in nearby Monterrey. The real estate boom that marked the 2000s was surging, and Jodi wanted to become an investor to capitalize on the soaring white-hot market. She says she took classes at Monterrey Peninsula College and learned about real estate.

By the summer of 2005, she and Darryl were ready for a change of scenery, so they moved south to Palm Desert, California, a city known for its punishing summertime heat and more comfortable winter climate that draws thousands of snowbirds every year. Also, Darryl's ex-wife was moving to the area at the same time, so it made sense to be in Palm Desert for when he had visitation rights with their son.

Jodi and Darryl bought a house together where little Jack would visit. Jodi and Jack grew closer, and she was a stepmother of sorts to the little boy. On one Father's Day, Jodi put her art skills to use by giving her lover a drawn family picture as a gift.

They bought a three-bedroom home with a swimming pool in June 2005, despite the fact that their finances were shaky, to say the least. Darryl didn't have a job at the time, and Jodi was working at a local California Pizza Kitchen and later took on a second restaurant job. Jodi had more than $10,000 in savings earlier in her relationship with Darryl, but she burned through it by the end of their time together.

She was paying half the mortgage, and had a new expense when she traveled to the San Diego area to get breast implants.

Then little Jack's mother suddenly decided to relocate to the Monterrey area—more than nine hours away—prompting them to reevaluate their decision to move to Southern California. Darryl began looking for work in Monterrey, and the relationship seemed to crumble day by day in the summer of 2006.

Darryl started noticing changes in Jodi around this time. She quit paying household bills, and her behavior grew strange. She ran up credit card debt and had trouble paying her half of the mortgage, now $2,800 a month.

She became more spiritual and started spending time with Mormon missionaries. Young Mormon men who were total strangers to Darryl were suddenly in his living room holding prayer sessions. Jodi scolded Darryl when he cursed.

They quit having sex. Jodi was saving herself for her husband, she said.

But it wasn't all bleak for Jodi. She had three new things in her life that brought her excitement: the Mormon church, a company called Prepaid Legal, and a man named Travis Victor Alexander.

4

"I'M TRAVIS ALEXANDER"

"**W**here do you see yourself in five years?"

The question was posed to Jodi from a 20-something co-worker at a California Pizza Kitchen.

"Real estate," Jodi replied. "What about you?"

Retirement, he said. The co-worker had what he considered a get-rich-quick scheme through a company called Prepaid Legal. He gave her a magazine and DVD about the company, and Jodi paid it no mind. She tossed the materials aside in a storage closet and forgot about them.

Months later—as things were falling apart with Darryl in 2006—Jodi was cleaning out the closet and stumbled upon the Prepaid Legal discs. She watched and became intrigued by the concept.

The technical term for the company's structure is "multi-level marketing." The best comparison is Amway. Generations of Americans are familiar with the aggressive sales tactics of Amway workers, who sign up salespeople for the product and ask them do the same to draw in other prospective clients. Prepaid Legal had a similar structure for its sales force, and Travis was one of its rising stars.

Jodi's first big introduction to the company was on a trip to the MGM Grand in Las Vegas in September 2006 for a Prepaid Legal convention that attracted thousands of people from all over the U.S. and Canada.

She carpooled to the event from California with two other Prepaid Legal devotees. After a couple days of chilling by the pool and meeting new people, Jodi and her friends had dinner at the Rainforest Cafe.

They settled up their check and were waiting outside the restaurant when Jodi saw a man from the corner of her eye. They exchanged looks.

His brisk walk and confidence stood out amid the crowds of people, the cacophony of slot machines, and the smell of stale cigarette smoke.

This guy is going somewhere, literally and figuratively, she thought. She was a little taken aback when he extended his hand to introduce himself.

"I'm Travis Alexander."

They immediately had a connection, and Travis gave Jodi his undivided attention as they walked through the casino and chatted. After exchanging some small talk and tidbits about Prepaid Legal, Travis invited her to an executive banquet that night.

He was an executive director at the time, entitling him to exclusive tickets to the event that Jodi could not have gotten given her newbie status in the organization.

The affair was intoxicating to her. She was no stranger to

high-end dinners, but for most of her life, she was the one serving the meals, not receiving them.

On top of that, the discussion of wealth was a little dizzying for Jodi. To succeed at Prepaid Legal, you needed to be an aggressive salesperson—always closing, the mantra goes—and the company wasn't shy about heaping honors on the most successful employees.

If you make $100,000 in a year, you get a ring. Pull in $250,000 and you get a diamond embedded in the ring. A half-million dollars and you get two diamonds.

It was a fun weekend for Jodi as she was introduced to a guy who clearly was into her. She and Travis talked about his love of Ultimate Fighting Challenge and the San Francisco 49ers. Even though Travis grew up in Southern California, where the San Diego Chargers and the Raiders were popular, he rooted for San Francisco because Steve Young was the star quarterback. Young is a Mormon who starred at BYU and is actually a descendant of Brigham Young.

They parted ways after the weekend but made sure to exchange numbers to meet up again, even though Jodi was still living with Brewer in what she said was a platonic arrangement. They talked on the phone for hours on end in the month or so that followed, then decided to meet up in Ehrenburg, Arizona, along the California-Arizona border, to see each other in person. Travis was living in Mesa at the time, and Jodi was still in California, so Ehrenburg was a good meeting point.

They went to a movie in nearby Blythe, California, watched game shows on the TV in their hotel room and had dinner at Sizzler.

They also hooked up for the first time.

They started kissing from the minute they walked into the hotel room. It escalated to grinding on each other fully clothed—what Jodi called the "Provo push," a maneuver that gets its name from the predominantly Mormon city in Utah that is home to BYU. The faith discourages sexual intimacy of any sort out of wedlock.

At this point, Travis was already trying to get Jodi to join the Mormon church, even sending missionaries to her house in Palm Desert.

By the end of the weekend, their intimacy had escalated far beyond just rubbing their bodies together. They performed oral sex on each other. They had breakfast at a truck stop restaurant and went home to their respective cities.

Jodi claimed at her trial that she felt used by Travis during the weekend, "like a prostitute." But at the same time, she could have just written Travis and the whole weekend off as a silly, passion-filled mistake. Of course, she didn't.

She called him Saturday when she was driving home. No answer. She called him again Sunday. No answer. She sent text messages on Monday. Travis was starting to see another side of Jodi, an obsessive one that would rear its head again.

5

THE MORMON COURTSHIP

*"No man for any considerable period can wear one face to himself
and another to the multitude without finally getting bewildered
as to which may be the true."*
—Nathaniel Hawthorne.

An overlooked fact about the relationship between Jodi and
Travis is that they knew each other for only 21 months.
They met in September 2006, and he was dead by June 2008.

The relationship between Jodi and Travis can essentially be
broken up into three acts. The first was the initial courtship
that included an introduction to the Mormon church and Prepaid Legal. That lasted from September 2006 until February
2007.

The second act was Travis and Jodi as boyfriend-girlfriend,
a period that covered five months, from February 2007 until
late June 2007.

The final act—reminiscent of a Shakespearean tragedy—
was the breakup period, during which they continued to see
each other for sexual trysts. It ended on that fateful, violent
day in Travis' bathroom, June 4, 2008.

Each facet of their relationship was intriguing in its own way, but the Mormon saga was especially fascinating. The story is a clash between the chaste values of the Mormon church and the innate sexual desires of a couple finding it increasingly difficult to resist each other.

Travis began talking up the Mormon church to Jodi almost immediately after they met at the Prepaid Legal event in Las Vegas. As they began their months-long courtship through a series of phone calls, text messages, and hotel hookups, Travis slowly began convincing Jodi that The Church of Jesus Christ of Latter-day Saints was the right religion for her. She considered herself an Evangelical Christian growing up, but was drawn to the Mormon faith—never mind the fact that at the time she was unmarried and living with Darryl Brewer, loved Starbucks, and was performing oral sex on Travis. All three would be considered violations of church doctrine—no living with a person of the opposite sex out of wedlock, no caffeine, and certainly no sex of any kind.

Jodi said Travis would always bring up anal sex to her. To him, anal and oral sex were acceptable under the Mormon faith because they did not involve vaginal intercourse. Jodi said that Travis had the "Bill Clinton version," where oral sex, well, wasn't really sex.

It was an utterly false rationalization. Chastity means chastity in the Mormon faith. No exceptions. Jodi also said Travis started sending photos of his erect penis to her via text message, causing her embarrassment on one evening as she had dinner with friends in California.

By November 2006, Jodi had decided she wanted to join the church. She said her parents, siblings, and extended family cautioned against the move, urging her to not jump so quickly into a religion that required so much dedication and commitment. It's not the type of religion that you dabble in, they warned.

She met with a church elder to discuss her willingness to adhere to the faith, including acceptance of the Book of Mormon, her belief that Joseph Smith was a prophet of God and her understanding of the law of chastity and other LDS tenets such as giving up alcohol, coffee, and tea.

There was a hitch, however. Jodi was still living with Darryl at the time, and Mormons are discouraged from living in the same house as someone of the opposite sex who isn't a family member or a marital partner.

They ran the situation by a church official, who made sure that she and Darryl were living in separate bedrooms and not intimately involved. She was allowed to join, and the induction was scheduled for November 26, 2006.

It was the Saturday after Thanksgiving, and the day Travis would baptize her.

Jodi described being nervous as hymns were sung and prayers were read, and a white-clad Travis stood in waist-high water in a font at the front of the church.

She entered the water, herself dressed in white. Travis dipped her down to perform the baptism. She was now a member of the Mormon church.

Jodi would later tell the jury at her trial what happened next, but the exact nature of the encounter and the veracity of the story is impossible to corroborate. She says she and Travis drove back to a house of a friend where they were staying. As they entered the bedroom, they began passionately kissing.

It became more intense with each intimate touch of their lips. Jodi says Travis then spun her around and bent her over the bed and lifted up her skirt, eventually removing her church clothes. He slid off her panties and proceeded to engage in anal sex. She says he ejaculated on her back, they kissed, and the tryst was over as suddenly as it had begun.

Their sexual relationship was not exclusive at this point as Travis wanted to see other women, so Jodi carried on with her life in California. She went on a couple dates with other men, but nothing serious came of them.

The LDS component of their relationship served as a juicy subplot throughout the entire case—at times playing out like a Mormon soap opera as young church members engaged in wholesome activities while simultaneously gossiping about friends fooling around in bed and breaking the law of chastity.

Some of the stories ended up being broadcast for a global audience during her trial. Travis dated a fellow Mormon named Deanna Reid before he met Jodi and they remained close until his death, with her adopting his dog after he was killed. Deanna and Travis dated from 2002 to 2005 but broke it off because he wasn't ready for marriage and she wanted to settle down.

During Jodi's trial, defense lawyer Kirk Nurmi pressed Reid for details about their level of intimacy. Reid was forced to uncomfortably admit in open court that she and Travis had sex several times. They confessed to their bishop, asked for forgiveness, and moved on with their lives.

Travis made it seem to friends that he was a loyal follower of the church's strict moral code, a virgin saving himself for marriage, but he clearly had sexual urges.

He tried to keep up the appearance with the series of Mormon women he dated over the years even as he lusted for what he called his "dirty little secret"—Jodi Arias. She was the femme fatale who caused him to stray far from his Mormon values, and who would ultimately cut his life tragically short.

6

LIGHTING THE FUSE

"Is this a lasting treasure, or just a moment's pleasure?"
—The Shirelles

When looking back at Jodi and Travis' relationship, think of a stick of dynamite. The fuse gets lit and slowly burns, crackling with greater intensity as it approaches the dynamite, then a thunderous explosion ending in a blood bath.

The fuse was lit during that glorious weekend in Las Vegas in 2006. It only burned faster as the months passed on.

It was now early February 2007. Jodi had known Travis for about five months—a period in which she was baptized into the Mormon faith, joined Prepaid Legal, and fell so hard for Travis that she was willing to engage in all sorts of sexual acts. Again, no one but Jodi and Travis know who was the sexual instigator throughout their time together. Jodi would claim Travis coerced her into the raunchiness, but it appeared clear both enjoyed it equally.

She was ready to take the relationship to the next level.

Jodi finished her restaurant shift in Palm Desert and got in her car and drove to Mesa. No phone calls, texts or emails to say she was coming—this was a completely unannounced trip.

She was going to surprise Travis. Jodi testified that Travis made a similar trip earlier, so she wanted to do the same.

They fooled around in his bedroom most of the weekend, watched TV, hung out with Travis' roommate, and surfed the Internet. The conversation eventually turned to dating—and doing so exclusively. They had seen other people in the early months of their courtship, and there was jealousy on both sides over the thought of either person being intimate with anyone else.

"When we became what I believed was exclusive it just seemed like the natural next step," Jodi would later say.

While they surfed the Internet, Jodi hit the back button to look at something again. Then she kept hitting the button on the browser until she went all the way back to Travis' MySpace page. It's not known if it was an accident or the work of a woman who was an admitted snoop, but she found some things she didn't like.

She saw an old email exchange between Travis and another woman, but it was before they started getting serious, so she ignored it. They were a couple now, no need to mess up a good thing with a guy she was already thinking about marrying.

Over the next couple months, Travis and Jodi carried on a long-distance relationship between Mesa and California, about four hours apart, seeing each other on a regular basis.

They couldn't spend Valentine's Day together because of their geographic limitations, but Travis sent her a gift, she says: a package containing some melted chocolate, a T-shirt, and pink shorts inscribed with Travis' name.

Jodi thought it was funny because Travis had joked he might do something like that. The package contained another surprise, Jodi claims: little boy's Spider-Man-themed underwear. Photos of the T-shirt and shorts with Travis' name on them were shown to jurors at her trial. The jury, however, never saw the mysterious comic book underwear that Jodi's defense lawyers hoped to bolster their claim that Travis was a pedophile.

In the spring of 2007, Jodi and Travis took a trip to the Midwest to visit Mormon holy sites in Missouri and Illinois before they went to a Prepaid Legal convention in Oklahoma City.

Despite the fact that they were an official item at the time, Jodi says Travis was closed-off during the trip and refused to give her much attention, in what she perceived as his unwillingness to be seen as her boyfriend in public. She said he continued to refuse to introduce her as his girlfriend as the weeks went on.

Her jealousy grew later in the trip when a drunken woman started causing a scene at the Sheraton where they were staying during the convention. The woman was bombed out of her mind, draping herself all over random men, and cracking jokes. It was such a scene that Jodi pulled out her phone to capture some video of it.

The woman was eventually drawn to Travis and started hanging on him. Jodi says Travis went along with it, and Jodi got mad. She retreated to a bathroom stall and cried.

They made up and went back to their respective homes.

Despite Jodi's perceived slights at the hands of Travis, the relationship moved along like most relationships do. There were more trips, even meeting the family.

Jodi got to meet Travis' grandmother Norma Sarvey during a visit to Riverside. He still wouldn't introduce her as his girlfriend, she said.

Jodi and Travis shared a desire to travel together. They were both big fans of a book called *1,000 Places to See Before You Die*, and they tried to cross off the easy ones on the list in their geographic area such as Sedona, Arizona, Carlsbad Caverns in New Mexico, and the Grand Canyon.

7

THE BREAKUP: JODI UNRAVELS

*"I love him. I could not possibly love him not,
though I wish I could stop."*

—Jodi Arias

Jodi and Travis broke up in late June 2007. She says he was cheating on her so she ended it. Travis' friends say he felt she was becoming increasingly obsessive and jealous.

In most breakups, couples want to get away from each other. They move out, avoid public places where they might see the other person, sometimes even relocate to different cities for a fresh start.

Not Jodi.

A few weeks after they broke up, she actually moved from California to Mesa to be closer to him.

She lived there until the spring of 2008—a tumultuous period of her life that she later described as a roller coaster of emotions. Passionate lovemaking sessions, followed by nasty fights. The fuse was burning really fast by now.

"I was making a string of bad choices during that time in my life," Jodi would tell jurors at her trial.

Jodi had all sorts of hard luck while in Mesa. She had a roommate right after moving to Arizona, but then the roommate ran off to Las Vegas with her boyfriend and got hitched. Jodi had to find a new place to live, and it just so happens, she found one only a few minutes from Travis' house.

He was a little upset and caught off-guard by the decision because it might have put them in the same Mormon ward. How could he possibly move on and find a nice companion at church events if Jodi was always lurking? Jodi made sure she ended up in a different singles ward, so everything was fine in that regard.

She was making questionable financial decisions at the time, struggling so badly to make payments on her 2004 Infiniti G-35 that she relinquished it to the dealership. Her restaurant jobs weren't paying much and she was running up debt with her parents and other family members.

To earn extra money, she would clean Travis' house.

Travis began dating a girl named Lisa Andrews after Jodi. He first met Lisa at church. She was Mormon, too. They talked at ward gatherings and later started texting and talking on the phone. They began seeing each other in July, right after the breakup with Jodi. Lisa was 19 at the time, about 10 years younger than Travis.

They dated off and on for roughly seven months, and drama seemed to follow them every step of the way. Travis had just turned 30 and kept telling Lisa that he wanted to get married— he was ready to give up the single life and settle down with a nice Mormon girl. Lisa wasn't quite ready for that, still less than two years out of high school.

She didn't know quite what to think when she heard a rumor going around her circle of Mormon friends and family: Travis was seeing someone else. It turned out to be Jodi. On top of that, he and Jodi had been taking out-of-town trips together in what Travis brushed off as innocent little excursions.

Lisa broke it off, but the always-persuasive Travis convinced her that they should give it another shot. They got back together but broke up again after Lisa said she became uncomfortable with Travis' unrelenting talk of marriage. She dumped him a second time, but again, they got back together.

Then, on December 8, 2007, Lisa got a disturbing email from an anonymous sender.

It read:

You are a shameful whore. Your Heavenly Father must be deeply ashamed of the whoredoms you've committed with that insidious man. If you let him stay in your bed one more time or even sleep under the same roof as him, you will be giving the appearance of evil. You are driving away the Holy Ghost, and you are wasting your time. You are also compromising your salvation and breaking your baptismal covenants. . . . You cannot be ashamed enough of yourself. You are filthy, and you need to repent and become clean in the eyes of God. Think about your future husband, and how you disrespect not only yourself, but him, as well as become clean in the eyes of God. Is this what you want for yourself? Your future, your salvation and your posterity is resting on your choices and actions.

She never could prove who sent it, but only one person came to mind: Jodi.

Things kept getting stranger.

On February 2, 2008, she and Travis were hanging out at his house one night when they heard a knock on the door. No one was there. They didn't think much of it, but later came to find the tires of Travis' car were slashed.

They called Mesa police but got sick of waiting for the cops to show up, so no police report was ever filed. No one could ever prove it was Jodi, but suspicions were aroused, and after the killing, friends were certain she was culprit.

It didn't stop there.

Jodi admits that she was a complete mess during the post-Travis breakup period, as marked by the stalking episodes and another time when she sneaked into Travis' house through the doggy door. In another previous stalking episode in August 2007, Lisa and Travis were at his house when Jodi showed up and peered through the window.

Her diary, obtained during the trial by ABC's *Good Morning America*, was clear proof of how increasingly unraveled she was becoming.

On August 2, shortly after Travis started dating Lisa, she wrote this:

I love him. I could not possibly love him not, though I wish I could stop. Turn it off like a lightswitch. Duct tape it down so it can't turn back on. Or better yet, just cut the circuit. Cut off its life source. Make it dead in a second. Lifeless. A meaningless network of wires that do and mean nothing.

In another entry, she wrote:

Well it's a good thing that nobody else reads this because I write right now that I love Travis Victor Alexander so completely that I don't know any other way to be. I wish I did because at times my heart is sick and saddened over all that has come to pass, I don't understand it and at times still have a hard time believing it. He makes me sick and he makes me happy. He makes me sad and miserable. And he makes me feel uplifted and beautiful. All in all I shouldn't be wording it as though he makes me feel those things. It all originates from within, all of my darkness is a result of my own creation, it is the fruit of my thoughts planted continually and with too much repetition.

I just wish I could die. I wish that suicide was a way out but it is no escape. I wouldn't feel any more pain.

She also fretted about her financial situation in the diary—and how she kept giving money to Travis even though she was short on money.

If you believe Jodi, Travis needed the cash because he was having financial troubles. His checking account was depleted, and she loaned him about $900 in January 2008 alone, she said.

There is some evidence of this in real estate documents in Maricopa County as he refinanced that year for extra cash.

Travis bought the house at 11428 East Queensborough in 2004 for $250,000, a nice deal for a new place with a stucco roof, three-car garage, two levels and located in a quiet neighborhood.

The value of his house soared in the real estate boom in the three years that followed—so much so that Travis was able to pocket about $80,000 through a mortgage refinance just two months before his death.

By late March 2008, Jodi was sure that she wanted out of Mesa—and away from Travis. She packed up her belongings into a U-Haul truck to move back home to Northern California.

She went to see Travis one last time, then drove away from his house in the dark of night. But she started getting sleepy and pulled off to the side of the road. She turned around and went back to Travis' home, unable to leave him just yet.

She needed a new car at this point, and Travis was trying to get rid of his BMW in favor of the more emission-friendly Prius. He and Jodi worked out a deal where she would take the car back to California and either sell it to a friend in the restaurant business or buy it from Travis. She was really going to move this time.

She placed her houseplants in the passenger seat of her U-Haul truck, fastening them with the seatbelt to make sure her proud possessions were secure. She hitched the BMW to the tow dolly and hit the road.

As she reached the freeway, something was wrong with the truck. She couldn't get any power; it felt like the BMW was a huge drag. Cars were whizzing past her, honking their horns as she bogged down the pace of the freeway. Smoke was pouring from the BMW. She exited off a ramp and found oil spraying everywhere from the engine compartment. She had left the car in first gear. It was now basically worthless—a used BMW with a destroyed engine or transmission that would cost thousands of dollars to fix.

She couldn't let Travis go emotionally or leave his orbit.

She went back and spent another night with Travis, then tried to leave again the next day. There was yet another problem: She forgot about the houseplants she'd left in the truck. These were the same plants she had owned since she lived in Palm Desert. They blossomed during her time with Travis, and she even moved them into his Mesa house because she didn't have the space at her apartment.

She opened the door to the U-Haul and the plants were wilted in the front seat. She left town and didn't see Travis again until the day she killed him.

8

A NEW BEGINNING

"Desperately trying to find out if my date has an axe
murderer penned up inside of her . . ."
—Travis Alexander

The year 2008 was supposed to be a new beginning for Travis. He was trying to put the Jodi period of his life behind him and find a nice Mormon girl he could settle down with. He was thrilled about the prospects of what the year would bring.

At the time, Travis was 30, a key turning point for people in the Mormon church. That is because 31 is an important age for those of the faith.

Members belong to wards based on where they live, and the wards are broken up into ones for singles and families. The distinction is pretty straightforward, but there is an exception. Once you turn 31, whether you are still single or not, you automatically join a family ward. Travis was coming up on this date at the end of July 2008, and he was giving every indication he was ready to settle down.

Three weeks before his death—on May 18, 2008—Travis wrote a blog post called "Why I want to marry a gold digger," a provocative headline that no doubt raised eyebrows among his friends in the Mormon church and at Prepaid Legal.

Travis didn't see the "gold digger" phrase as a negative. He noted that it wasn't about material wealth. He wanted something deeper.

"I couldn't think of a better phrase to describe what I desire in an Eternal Companion," he wrote. "I want someone to love me for the Gold that is with in me and is willing to dig with me to extract it."

It was an introspective post in which he reflected on his single years, joked about how he had become one of the most eligible Mormon bachelors around, looked ahead to married life, and noted how his grandmother was only five years older than his current age when she had grandchildren.

There were even some delusions of self-grandeur as he imagined himself as some "dangerously handsome tycoon in *Time* magazine as one of the world's most eligible bachelors."

> Then I turned 30. As I tend to do, I did a little soul searching and realized that I was lonely. A quote from David O. McKay kept haunting me. 'No success can compensate for failure in the home.' I was a different type of homeless, one with just as few legitimate excuses as the other type bumming for change at a freeway off ramp.

He continued writing.

> Around then I realized it was time to adjust my priorities and date with marriage in mind. Not to ask someone on a date

because I planned on marrying them, but to date someone to look for the possibility of marriage with them.

This type of dating to me is like a very long job interview and can be exponentially more mentally taxing. Desperately trying to find out if my date has an axe murderer penned up inside of her . . .

To Travis, Marie "Mimi" Hall epitomized the type of woman who was marriage material. They met after she gave a talk at a Sunday service, and Travis approached her afterward to compliment her on the sacrament.

They went on three dates in early 2008 while Travis was still seeing Jodi on the side. Mimi and Travis hung out at Mormon church events for young singles, such as ice-skating and trips to a lake for a barbecue. They went to dinner and sipped hot chocolate at a Barnes and Noble on their first date. They went to a pottery class. They went rock-climbing at a gym in Tempe. They saw each other at church events, including a book and movie club that Hall organized.

They were part of a group of twenty-something Mormons who once went on an overnight camping trip—women slept in cabins, men stayed outside. No chance for any shenanigans that way.

It was about as wholesome of a relationship as Travis could have ever imagined—really the antithesis of his rocky romance with Jodi. Mimi was a lifelong Mormon and a BYU graduate. Jodi was a high school dropout and a convert to Mormonism. Mimi had a good relationship with her mother. Jodi did not. Mimi ended up working in banking at JP Morgan Chase. Jodi once waited tables at Denny's. Mimi was a more conservative brunette whose physical appearance was strikingly different from the often-platinum blond vixen Jodi presented herself as.

But Mimi was the first to admit that there was no real spark in her relationship with Travis, and it became mostly platonic. They stayed in touch via email, text messages, and phone calls and saw each other at various church events.

In the months before his death, Travis reached out to Mimi with a tempting offer. He had a free work trip to Cancun coming up on June 10, and he invited her to come along. Mimi thought about it, and was a little apprehensive. Travis assuaged her concerns by reminding her that they would be staying with a Mormon family, and that Mimi would be sharing a room with the family's daughter.

So she took him up on the offer and booked the trip. They talked on June 2 about the vacation—excited at the prospect of escaping the stifling Arizona summer heat for a beachside paradise.

According to authorities, Jodi had already begun plotting his murder, fuming with jealousy.

She and Travis got in a vicious fight on May 26. The exact nature of the spat is not completely known, but it's clear that by this point Travis was really becoming fed up with Jodi's erratic behavior and stalking. The feud played out largely over text message as Travis fumed over Jodi making a comment on a friend's Facebook page that referenced the Will Ferrell movie *Anchorman*.

He called her a "sociopath," "evil" and a "whore" and said she was the worst thing that ever happened to him.

The conversation could be interpreted two ways, and lawyers on both sides sought to use the fight to their advantage at the trial. Prosecutors said it was the tipping point that drove

Jodi to kill him. The defense said it showed how much Travis verbally abused Jodi and used her for sex.

Two days later, on May 28, police in Yreka responded to a report of a burglary at the home of Sonny and Caroline Allen— Jodi's grandparents and where she was living at the time.

It was an unusual break-in and theft. The thieves got away with $30 in cash, a DVD player, a stereo, and a .25-caliber handgun. The robbers did not bother to take other guns, nor did they grab any of the spare change that was left nearby.

Police later came to believe that it was an inside job, carried out by Jodi to secure a handgun for the killing, and she made it look like some random burglary. No one has ever been arrested for the theft, and Jodi to this day denies having had anything to do with it.

The same caliber gun was used to shoot Travis in the head. The weapon has never been found.

9

BUBBLE BATHS, PORN, AND PHONE SEX

"Is she perverted like me?
Would she go down on you in a theater?"
—Alanis Morissette

One month before Travis' body was discovered, he and Jodi had a late-night phone call that provides one of the most revealing glimpses into their relationship, while also portraying the duality of Travis. He was clearly a man conflicted and torn internally, overcome with his sexual urges for Jodi while at the same time trying to be a good Mormon.

Jodi was in a bedroom in her grandparents' house in Yreka, California, and Travis was home in Mesa. Jodi made sure to record the conversation, she says, at Travis' urging. The call was played in open court during her trial, eliciting cringes from the gallery and Jodi herself during the X-rated, hour-plus chat. Jurors squirmed uncomfortably in their chairs.

The call contained no outward signs of tension or strife in their relationship. In fact, just the opposite. Travis was telling friends at the time that he had grown frustrated with his "stalker ex-girlfriend," but he gave no sign of any issues he had with Jodi on this particular night, on this particular raunchy call.

Jodi later portrayed herself as a victim of Travis' unwanted sexual advances, but on the phone call seemed absolutely in to every dirty pornographic fantasy that Travis wanted to play out with her. Both appeared to have their own perversions.

The conversation is also insightful because it is a rare case where the world got to hear Travis' own words after his death—not just the many one-sided accounts from Jodi that were broadcast over the last five years in TV interviews, news accounts and during her trial.

While there is little doubt that Travis was serious about the Mormon religion and an inspiration to people at his church and job, the call makes it clear that he had a weakness for sex that ran counter to his religious beliefs.

The call was basically a summation of their sex life as they reflected on everything they did together. It included their recollections of passionate grinding in the Ehrenburg, Arizona hotel room. It went on in graphic detail: Jodi introducing lubricant to Travis to ease the pain of their anal sex encounters; his "superhuman" stamina during intercourse; lovemaking during a candle-lit bubble bath; kinky acts such as him giving her oral sex with a Tootsie Pop; and makeup sex that veered into the angry side but was no less incredibly satisfying.

There were also some subtle hints of jealousy and obsessiveness on both of their parts during the call—and plenty of irony. At one point, Jodi talked about how she was blossoming sexually as she approached her 30s, but how she was still a little shy.

"I'm all for the wild streak, but I don't broadcast it to the whole world," Jodi says on the call that ultimately was heard by thousands of people around the globe.

It also seemed like Jodi was fishing at various points in the conversation. She asked about Cancun, his other planned trips, and how they hoped to spend some time together visiting Crater Lake and a Shakespeare festival in the near future. Travis complimented her on what an "A-plus ass" she has.

"You're an A-plus," Jodi promptly replied, seemingly hoping to elicit something from Travis about his similar feelings for her.

Travis didn't take the bait. Instead, he responded with a raunchy reference to an act of anal and oral sex: "I'd love doing it to you."

Later, Jodi turned the conversation to marriage. She commented on how the two were eventually going to wed other people but that it would be difficult for many other Mormon men and women to match the kinkiness they had enjoyed together. She teed it up perfectly for Travis, who had every opportunity to say something like: "You're right—I won't find a Mormon girl like you, Jodi. I want to be with you."

He didn't.

"I'm gonna tie you to a tree and put it in your ass, by the way," he said.

"Oh my gosh, that is so debasing. I like it," Jodi responded lightheartedly.

Travis then described that he wanted her to be blindfolded during the encounter, and how he wanted to make an amateur porn video out of it. Jodi was now getting turned on.

"Oh my gosh, you are full of ideas," she said.

Travis clearly viewed Jodi as a girl who could bring his pornographic fantasies to life. She had everything he wanted: fake breasts, a petite body, dyed platinum blond hair, and an unfettered desire to do whatever he wanted in the sack.

His vision for the amateur movie went like this: He wanted

to put on a park ranger outfit and bust Jodi for some only-in-a-porno type of infraction such as being nude in public, Travis explained on the call.

The only way out of a ticket would be for Jodi to please him sexually. Travis also wanted to get pictures of him ejaculating inside her in what he envisioned as "legitimate porn."

Jodi was really getting turned on by now. He talked about her body, her nipples, her genitalia, how she was the "prototype of sluttiness," and "made to fuck."

Jodi feigned masturbation during the call, commenting on how Travis made her feel like the "most freaking beautiful woman on the whole planet."

Jodi did draw some kind words out of Travis, she talked about her MySpace profile photos and how she doesn't look good in some pictures.

"No, you're pretty," Travis replied.

"You are just so attractive . . . I've never seen you look bad in my life," he said, prompting Jodi to play the modesty card. She said that's not true, she has looked unattractive plenty of times during their relationship.

"There have been many times when you looked miserable and, I like, raped you," Travis replied.

At one point, Jodi got off, and Travis loved every bit of it. She later claimed she was faking the orgasm, testifying in court that it would have been impossible to achieve climax with only one hand. Her other hand was holding the phone.

"You make me feel so dirty," she said on the call.

Travis commented on how hot it was to hear Jodi climaxing, noting how she sounded like a 12-year-old girl achieving her first orgasm.

"What are we gonna do with ourselves," Jodi said. "We are just horny toads."

She had another apparent orgasm later in the call that occurred simultaneous to Travis doing the same.

"If I had a sperm bank I could retire off this load," he told her.

The talk then pivoted to music, pop culture, film, and some spirited debate about superhero movies, Spider-Man vs. Batman, that kind of thing. Travis and Jodi both liked to sing, so he broke out into the Grateful Dead favorite "Truckin'" and they belted out the Alanis Morissette number "Head Over Feet" together.

The entirety of the conversation really encapsulated their relationship together. It was a mixture of sex, laughs, jealousy and obsessiveness, social media, marriage talk and reminiscing about their times together—the good times, the not so good times, and the upcoming trip to Cancun that Travis would never make.

The call eventually became a key piece of evidence at Jodi's trial, including the part where she and Travis recalled how he once woke her up in the middle of the night and began administering oral sex not long after she had gotten a Brazilian bikini wax.

One of Jodi's defense lawyers insisted at her trial that his comments on the call were not those "of a man who was being relentlessly stalked and does not want to have any contact," as authorities contended in their case against Jodi.

In addition, the last three minutes of the call effectively summed up what was going on between Jodi and Travis—firmly in the category of "you can't make this stuff up."

Jodi made one last attempt to draw some affection out of

Travis by telling him he was cute, but he didn't go there. Instead, Travis appeared to grow tired of talking.

As his yawning grew more incessant, Jodi suggested that they try to "astral project" to find each other in their sleep—a reference to an out-of-body experience in which people believe they can be transported to a different place through their minds.

And Jodi did a rendition of "You Oughta Know," the Morissette song that has become an anthem for an entire generation of scorned women. It was a prescient reminder of Jodi's own anger toward Travis that would rear its head a few weeks later.

"Now every time I scratch my nails down someone else's back I hope you feel it," she sang. "I hope you feel it."

10

THE ROAD TRIP

*"Nothing behind me, everything ahead of me,
as is ever so on the road."*

—Jack Kerouac

Three weeks later, Jodi took a road trip. It was a bizarre excursion, covering 3,000 miles, spanning four states and including visits to four of her current and former lovers. One of them would be Travis.

The trip began in Yreka, California. The first leg of the journey was to the airport in nearby Redding.

At Budget Rent A Car, she told the man at the counter that she was embarking on a small, local trip. It was the first of many lies. He offered a red car, but she refused, saying she didn't want anything too bright in color that might attract attention from the police.

She accepted a white Ford Focus, an unassuming compact car that would blend into the rest of the traveling public, and drove away. She headed south toward the Pacific Coast, winding past the breathtaking views of redwoods, ocean and mountains.

Her first order of business was to visit her old boyfriend, Darryl Brewer. He was living in the Monterrey area at the time and Jodi dropped in to say hello, saying she was on a trip to visit friends. She had breakfast with him and his son while making a strange request that seemed completely out of the blue: She needed gas cans. Jodi also went to a Wal-Mart, and bought another container for about $12, but she said she later returned it. Authorities found no proof of such a return.

Brewer lent her two 5-gallon containers, and she was on her way. To this day, Brewer has never fully explained why he provided her the cans, or if he asked her why she needed them in a state like California that is dotted with thousands of gas stations. Police said she needed a way to get in and out of Arizona without having to stop for fuel, just another part of her plan to avoid detection.

She kept driving south, to the Los Angeles area. She slept in her car when she got tired and eventually made it to an Arco station in Pasadena. She not only filled up the car, but filled up the gas cans, too.

A few hours later, Jodi's cell phone went dead—no activity at all for more than 12 hours. This is a woman whose cell phone was practically attached to her hip. She was a prolific texter, she recorded entire conversations with her phone and even shot self-portraits during her road trip, but she said she misplaced her charger around the time she got to Arizona. Prosecutors said it was a lie. They contended that she turned her phone off so that law enforcement couldn't track her whereabouts during her murderous trip through the Southwest.

Jodi arrived at Travis' house at about 4 a.m. on June 4. But this was not a normal trip where the traveler calls ahead and lets their friend know what time they are arriving. Jodi showed up completely unannounced, according to police. She says Travis begged her to come.

She didn't bother knocking on the door or ringing the doorbell.

She knew his garage code—0187—so she opened the door and went into the house. She walked quietly, not knowing if Travis was sleeping or if his roommates were around. She crept up on him as he was in his office watching goofy You-Tube videos of people with tin foil on their heads, oblivious to the fact that Jodi was there staring at him. She stood there for about 30 seconds, and finally called attention to her appearance.

Travis was clearly surprised. But they had done this before, and Jodi had a good enough cover story about her road trip that it didn't register to Travis what was really going on in her head or that this would ultimately be the last day of his life.

Over the next roughly 14 hours, the two would surf the Internet, nap and have sex, punctuated by both taking nude photos of each other. Jodi then killed him, hurriedly cleaned up and split, leaving behind a gruesome scene that wouldn't be found for five days. Yet she didn't behave like a traumatized victim of a brutal attack. Instead, she continued on her unusual road trip, and immediately began working on an alibi.

Her license plate was her first issue. Authorities say she removed the back plate at some point during her trip, presumably to avoid detection given the abundance of surveillance cameras along the route. In her haste to place the plate back on the car, she put it on upside down, prosecutors said. Jodi had a different story. She said that during a stop at a Starbucks, an unruly group of skateboarders messed with the plates.

Jodi was still carrying the gun that she fired at Travis during their altercation. She said she dumped it in the desert somewhere, but only vaguely recalls any other details of the attack and aftermath.

From there, it was on to Salt Lake City to see her budding love interest, Ryan Burns. Jodi met Ryan at a Prepaid Legal conference, and they struck up a long-distance relationship in their few months of knowing each other, exchanging hundreds of instant messages during lengthy Internet chats.

Jodi was supposed to meet Ryan in Salt Lake City sometime Wednesday—the same day she had killed Travis. But by Wednesday night, when she still wasn't there, he called her on her cell phone and it went straight to voicemail. He was a little worried; it was strange for her not to show up like that.

He finally got a call from a disoriented and frazzled Jodi around 11 p.m. Wednesday. She had all sorts of excuses. She lost her cell phone charger. She went the wrong way on the freeway. She slept in her car. She finally showed up the next morning.

Jodi was going to accompany Ryan to a Prepaid Legal meeting, and she agreed to follow him in her rental car. After she pulled away from his house, Jodi saw the flashing lights on a police car. She was already jittery and now she was being confronted by a cop. Had she already been caught? Was she getting arrested for Travis' killing?

A West Jordan police officer walked up to the car. He started asking about why her license plate was upside down. Jodi explained it as a goof by her friends—they must have been playing a prank on her. She got off with a verbal warning.

Later in the trip, Jodi and Ryan ended up in his bedroom. It got a little hot and heavy as they made out. He commented on her bandaged hands as she caressed his body. He kissed her stomach, noticing that the "six-pack abs" she had been boasting in their Internet chats were no joke. When she climbed on top of him, he finally pulled back, telling her that as a Mormon, he couldn't take it any further.

Ryan said later that one thing in particular nagged at him during the sexually charged encounter.

"What happened to her hands?"

She said she cut them on a broken glass at her job at Margaritaville in California. She kept saying she had to get going to make it in time for her shift.

Yet there's not even a Margaritaville in Yreka. She did have a job in town, but at a different Mexican restaurant, so why lie? At the time, Ryan had no idea she wasn't being truthful.

The visit was so quick, Ryan didn't think much of it. Jodi stayed a little while longer and finally headed back home to return the rental car.

She gassed up in Winnemucca, Nevada, got some food at an In-N-Out Burger and dropped off the car at the Redding airport. She had put 2,834 miles on the car.

A few things seemed out of place for the Budget staff. Jodi was supposed to be taking a local trip, but traveled nearly 3,000 miles. She rented the car as a blonde, but returned it as a brunette. She had changed her appearance.

The car had some suspicious signs as well. The worker noticed red stains on all the seats—he thought it might be Kool-Aid. And all of the floor mats were gone.

11

"HER NAME IS JODI"

Many murder cases require months of stealth detective work to determine the culprit. It's never as easy as it seems on TV, where cases are conveniently solved by the end of an hour-long *Law and Order* or *CSI* episode.

But in the death of Travis, it took only minutes to pinpoint Jodi as a prime suspect.

The new woman in Travis' life, Mimi Hall, helped figure it out. It was just days before their trip to Cancun and she hadn't heard a word. She repeatedly texted him. Calls went straight to voicemail. She was scared for Travis, even more so when she heard from friends that some mysterious woman was stalking him. The days came and went.

Here it was, one day before their trip and she hadn't heard a peep from him. Something was up.

Friends and work colleagues of Travis were also puzzled.

The first sign of trouble came at 7 p.m. on the evening he was killed. It was an hour and a half after Jodi jabbed a knife in his heart and shot him in the head, and Travis was supposed to lead an important conference call for Prepaid Legal.

Chris Hughes, a Prepaid Legal colleague and one of Travis' best friends, was scheduled to be on it, but Travis never called in. In the next few days, Travis' cell phone was flooded with text messages and voicemails, from friends, roommates, and even Jodi as she concocted her alibi.

Mimi decided she had to go to Travis' home in Mesa. She was so worried that she called her mother on the drive over to calm her nerves.

She arrived at the home and repeatedly pounded on the door and rang the doorbell. She saw his pug-mix dog Napoleon excitedly jumping up and down at the entryway, but no sign of Travis.

She went home and emailed Travis. Her fears grew with each minute. She then contacted her friend Michelle Lowery and they went to his house again, this time around 10 p.m. They knocked together. Nothing.

They reached out to more of Travis' friends and finally tracked down one who had the code to his garage.

They typed it into the keypad—0187. As they made their way into the house, a foul stench quickly overpowered them.

By the time they got to his bedroom, it was clear that something bad had happened. Blood was on the floors, the smell even more powerful.

In the bathroom, there he was: Travis' bloated, naked corpse stuffed into his shower. Mimi frantically dialed 911.

"Oh my god," she said in a panicked voice.

"What's going on?" the female dispatcher said.

"A friend of ours is dead in his bedroom," she said.

The dispatcher scrambled officers to the home and assured Mimi and her friends that help was on the way.

The dispatcher kept Mimi on the line as officers sped toward the scene, getting as much information as she could about how Travis could have suffered such a horrible death.

"Has he been depressed at all? Thinking of committing suicide, anything like that?" the dispatcher asked.

"He's been really depressed because he broke up with this girl. And he was all upset about that, but I don't think he'd actually kill himself over that," Mimi said.

"Had he been threatened by anybody recently?"

"Yes, he has. He has an ex-girlfriend that's been bothering him and following him and slashing his tires and things like that."

"And do you know the ex-girlfriend's name?"

Mimi couldn't remember the name of the supposed stalker. She just knew that Travis was having some relationship issues. She asked her friends who had accompanied her to the house, and someone in the background chimed in. Then came the damning moment.

"Her name is Jodi," Mimi said.

There it was. Just a few minutes into the call, with police not even at the scene, and friends armed with a few basic details about Travis' recent troubles had pinpointed a suspect.

"OK, so last weekend, his stalker, he told her he never wanted to see her again. Had a big confrontation. And that's all we know," Mimi told the dispatcher.

The call ended shortly after. Police may not have known it yet, but they had their prime suspect.

Mimi's next days, and those of the others who discovered the body, were filled with horror and confusion, grilling by police and questions about what occurred, with the thoughts of Jodi always on their minds.

A few days later, Mimi attended Travis' memorial service. Among the crowd of mourners, one woman stood out.

"Are you Mimi Hall?" the stranger said, introducing herself. "I'm Jodi Arias."

12

THE INVESTIGATION

*"You won't answer my calls, you change your number.
I mean, I'm not gonna be ignored, Dan!"*
—*Fatal Attraction*

Many killers do things in predictable and secretive ways to cover their tracks. They go underground. They flee to Mexico or some extradition-free country. They try to keep their mouths shut and most definitely do nothing to arouse suspicion.

Not Jodi. She had to be part of it, still, even after his death, drawn to Travis and everything that involved him.

Mesa Police Detective Esteban "Steve" Flores got the call just as he had begun analyzing the horrific scene. It was a message from a woman named Jodi Arias who wanted to inquire about the killing.

Flores went on to pull an all-nighter and got sidetracked with the immediate demands of the scene. He is a soft-spoken veteran police detective, a stout man known for his careful, methodical work at every crime scene.

The next day, he got another message from the same woman. Jodi definitely wasn't hiding.

In fact, she was overly chatty. It was the first installment in her ever-shifting alibis.

She inquired about the crime, offered her assistance, asked about the murder weapon, and described her relationship with Travis, all largely unsolicited information.

She provided all sorts of little clues and tidbits about Travis and his home. He had a king-size bed, maybe it was a California king, she said. He slept on Egyptian cotton sheets.

Jodi told Flores she looked back at her phone records to see the last time she spoke to Travis. She described how he'd never lock the doors, and how she gave him grief about it.

"Maybe you can't talk about this but was there any kind of weapon used? Was there a gun?" she asked, fishing for anything to find out if the authorities were onto her.

Yes, Flores said, but he didn't tip his hand. He asked her if Travis had a gun or any weapons in his house. "His two fists," she said.

Despite everyone pointing to Jodi from the minute the body was discovered, police proceeded at a deliberate pace before actually putting her in handcuffs about a month later.

All of Travis' friends saw her as the prime suspect from the minute police affixed yellow tape to the perimeter of the property and began examining the bathroom and house for forensic clues.

But Flores and his colleagues still had a lot of work to do to build the case; the foundation was there with Jodi as a possible culprit, but they had to build a house on top of the foundation.

Police quickly interviewed Mimi Hall and Travis' two roommates, Enrique Cortez and Zachary Billings, to make sure none of them had a particular beef with Travis.

Investigators thought it was odd that his roommates had no idea Travis' bloated corpse was stuffed into the shower in the days after Jodi killed him. A stench from the body was present throughout the house, but Zachary and Enrique didn't think much of it and were so busy with their jobs, church, and girlfriends that they weren't home much anyway.

Enrique remembered smelling it, but it was a bachelor pad. For all he knew, Travis left some dirty dishes in his room before he went to Mexico. They never imagined that the smell came from his decomposing body just a few feet away behind Travis' bedroom door.

Leads and tips started coming in to police. They had to chase down each one and cross them off their list, a time-consuming task for the handful of officers working the case.

One anonymous caller phoned police to say they needed to look at a man named Dustin Thompson.

Dustin and his wife, Ashley, an employee at a Dillard's distribution center, were seeing their marriage fall apart. Ashley was friends with Travis. She had known him for about three years and had visited his house to watch UFC matches on a Wednesday night in May.

The caller notified police that Dustin somehow knew about the killing the day the body was discovered and went to the house to see what was going on with all the officers at the scene.

As it turns out, the tip was bogus and Dustin had nothing to do with the slaying. But police had to follow the tip and dozens of others regardless.

As Mesa cops awaited forensic results, Flores, the lead detective, kept in close contact with Jodi. The circumstantial evidence clearly pointed to her, but they wanted iron-clad proof.

Almost everyone who knew Travis was convinced who did it. No doubt. It had to be Jodi.

They had been creeped out by her bizarre behavior at various times and heard the stories from Travis about Jodi's stalking.

One friend even told police that Jodi had been "acting very *Fatal Attraction*" lately, referring to the film starring Glenn Close as an obsessed mistress whose heightening obsession with a married man ends in murder.

"There's an old saying that, if someone is just not acting right, look into it," Flores would later say.

The detective began piecing together clues as Jodi tried to put the pieces of her own life back together.

She tried to resume her activities in Yreka, but it wasn't easy because she had to carry on the outward appearance of a mourner while simultaneously dealing with the psychological trauma of knowing she had just killed the love of her life, the man she thought she'd marry someday. She cried for days.

She went to work at a Mexican restaurant in Yreka. She updated her MySpace page to say she "missed Travis. See you soon, my friend, but not soon enough," while also posting a photo gallery of her trips and times with him. As she flew back to California from Arizona after attending Travis' memorial service, she flirted with the guy sitting next to her on the plane and got his number, calling him after getting home.

She even wrote letters of condolence to Travis' family and sent a bouquet of white irises to Travis' beloved grandmother, Norma Sarvey, who raised him and inspired him so much.

"Travis always told me he liked the name Iris for a girl. . . . If I ever have a son I'll name him Alexander," she wrote in her diary.

On the whole, Jodi did quite well handling the situation and moving on, or at least making it look that way.

Her mother said the death of Travis brought her and Jodi closer, and she was finally starting to see positive changes in her daughter.

Maybe there was a silver lining to all of this, her mother thought.

"Just this last couple weeks since Travis' death has been the best relations that we've had in our whole life," Sandy Arias would later say during questioning by police. "Maybe this death has made her see that life is short and you can't be that way. And it's changing her."

At the same time, Jodi was also playing the role of sleuth. She would call Flores to get updates on the investigation and offer up stories that puzzled him.

She would leave him casual voicemails on his mobile phone.

"Hi Detective Flores. This is Jodi Arias calling in regard to Travis Alexander," she said in one message. "It's Saturday, not exactly sure what time, maybe you're off. I hope you're enjoying your day off. If you could give me a call back, my phone number is ***-***-****."

As she was leaving her message, forensic experts were analyzing the evidence. On June 26, 2008 the reports came back: The bloody palm print on the wall was Jodi's. One week later, on July 3, the DNA samples taken from the scene matched up to Jodi.

A few weeks earlier, Jodi and Travis' other friends voluntarily provided police saliva samples for DNA comparisons.

Flores shared his findings with the Maricopa County Attorney's Office, and prosecutors presented the case to a grand jury.

The panel indicted Jodi on July 9, 2008, the same day she celebrated her 28th birthday. It was now time to take Jodi into custody.

Jodi was at her grandparents' three-bedroom house when Mesa Police joined by deputies with the Siskiyou County Sheriff's Department showed up and slapped the cuffs on her.

Jodi was under arrest.

13

"I DON'T EVEN HURT SPIDERS"

"I think you're not grasping the reality of the situation."
—Detective Rachel Blaney
of the Siskiyou County Sheriff's Department

The date was July 15, 2008. It was the culmination of the most tumultuous period of Jodi's life.

In the span of 45 days, she had killed her lover in gruesome fashion, skipped town, hooked up with a new guy, mourned the loss of Travis, even sent his family condolence cards.

Now she was in a nondescript interrogation room in Yreka. Most people are nervous in this situation, rattled by the mere sight of handcuffs on their wrists, fearful about their lives being shattered once the authorities figure out what they did.

But Jodi seemed to have different coping mechanisms. She tried small talk with a female officer, asking if she was from Arizona. Then she complained about the temperature in the room. It's too cold, she said. She wondered where her purse was.

Here she was, locked up for what could be an eternity, and Jodi begged Flores for a sweater and inquired about her handbag.

"Any way you can turn the heat up in here or like, do you have a sweater I can borrow or something?" she asked Flores.

"I don't have any sweaters," he shot back.

They had a few back-and-forths that were fairly routine for police interrogations, and then Flores laid down the gauntlet.

"Everybody is saying, I don't understand what happened to Travis. I don't know who killed him. But you need to look at Jodi. And sometimes the simplest answers are the correct ones. And that's one of the reasons I started looking at you a little bit closer and over the last month or so I've gotten into Travis' life, talked to all his friends, his family. I got a really good understanding of who he is now. And I got a very good understanding of your relationship with him. And I'm just putting two and two together . . . and it kind of matches."

Whatever Jodi had told herself in the month since Travis' death, it surely set in by now that she was in trouble.

It wasn't the kind of interrogation you see on a TV drama where a defendant is standoffish, gives quick, one-word answers and demands for a lawyer to be present.

Jodi rambled on in long answers as detectives tried to sort out the truth. Jodi talked at length about her relationship with Travis, their beliefs in the Mormon faith, his desire to meet a nice Mormon girl, and her supposed adherence to the Ten Commandments. She tried to make sense of her relationship with Travis for Flores.

But what Flores really wanted was a confession. Police had all the physical evidence they needed by this point, and seemed to have motive figured out: jealousy. The murder weapon was a mystery, although the break-in at her grandparents' house provided ample circumstantial evidence.

So for two days, Flores and other officers threw everything they could at Jodi, alternating between good cop, bad cop, and father confessor. On the first day, Flores started off by questioning her gently, but slowly lost his patience as Jodi's responses meandered.

"He liked you, he loved you. He wanted to be with you but he was reluctant to make a commitment first off. And he truly didn't think that you were marriage material," Flores said. "And I don't know why not. I mean, I see you, you're a wonderful girl. You're struggling, you're trying to make your way through life and I don't see why you guys couldn't have made it, you know?"

"I think we just, we have very different philosophies," Jodi said.

Finally, Flores had enough. It was time to throw his trump card down on the table.

"What if I could show you proof you were there?" Flores asked.

"How?" Jodi said.

"Would that change your mind?"

"I wasn't there."

"You need to be honest with me Jodi."

"I was not at Travis' house."

"You were at Travis' house and you guys had a sexual encounter which there's pictures. And I know you know there's pictures because I have them. I will show them to you, OK? So, what I'm asking you is for you to be honest with me. I know you were there."

"Are you sure those pictures aren't from another time?" Jodi asked.

"Positive."

She continued to insist that she was not there, despite Flores saying he had reams of evidence proving otherwise.

"Jodi, this is over. This is absolutely over. You need to tell me the truth," Flores said.

"Listen, the truth is I did not hurt Travis."

She kept lying, even going so far as to offer up this bold statement: "Listen, if I'm found guilty, I don't have a life. I'm not guilty. I didn't hurt Travis. If I hurt Travis, I would beg for the death penalty."

"I don't even hurt spiders," she added.

Flores decided to increase the pressure on Jodi by telling her that he was going to bring pictures showing what happened. Before he left, he offered a parting shot: "Tell me exactly what happened because, you know what, I think your mom and your dad really deserve the truth. They're gonna be asking. . . . 'What was going through your mind and what caused you do to this?' It happened. And I can prove it happened and there's no doubt in my mind, and there is absolutely no doubt in anybody's mind who is investigating this that you were there and that you did this. But I'll let you think about that OK? And I'm gonna go look for some pictures . . . and I'll be right back."

"Detective, I'm not a murderer," Jodi insisted.

Flores wrapped up the conversation by explaining the process for defendants in her situation, including bail hearings, extradition to Arizona, and limited contact with family.

He pushed a few more times to get her to confess, but she didn't bite. Jodi asked about whether Travis' family or the public knew she had been arrested. Then came an odd request.

"This is a really trivial question and it's gonna reveal how shallow I am. But before they book me, can I clean myself up a little bit?" Jodi asked.

She wanted to go the bathroom. Flores said yes—but the handcuffs were staying on.

"Do you know I'm not, like, violent, or am gonna run. It's Yreka."

Flores left the room, but kept the video surveillance camera on as Jodi stayed there by herself with nothing but a water bottle and her thoughts.

Usually in these situations, criminal suspects will shrug, sigh, mope and show expressions of anger over their predicament.

Jodi's was still worried about her appearance. Still handcuffed, she got on the floor, dropped her head down and pulled it back swiftly to fluff her hair.

"You could have at least done your makeup," she said aloud to herself. "Gosh."

Later, she broke into song. She belted out a verse from a Dido ballad called "Here With Me."

"*I didn't hear you breathe/I wonder how I am still here. And I don't want to move a thing/it might change my memory.*"

She shuffled her water bottle to the left and right on the table in front of her, then picked at the label.

"*And I won't go. And I can't hide. And I can't breathe until you're resting here with me.*"

Later, a completely different song choice: "*O! Holy Night! The stars are brightly shining.*"

She chuckled to herself and continued with the song. "*He knows our needs, hear the angel voices. . . . O night when Christ was born.*"

She then cried.

At another point, she raised her arms and placed her hands behind her head, stretching her torso. She inspected a trash can. Then she went to the wall, placed her head on the floor, and did a headstand.

Jodi was later booked into the system and spent her first night in jail, but detectives took another crack at her crumbling story the next day. Now wearing an orange prison jumpsuit and handcuffs and still alone in the room, Jodi added to the soundtrack of her incarceration, this time the Bette Midler favorite, "The Rose."

"Just remember in the winter, far beneath the bitter snow, lies the seed."

Flores sent in another investigator to work on Jodi, and the good cop/bad cop game elevated. Detective Rachel Blaney of the Siskiyou County Sheriff's Department entered and unlocked the handcuffs, noting that "these types of cuffs aren't the most comfortable."

"Do you think they're really designed for comfort?" Jodi asked.

"They're not. OK, you're not going to give us any problems being out of the cuffs. You really don't look like the type that would."

Blaney then took on a soothing, almost mother-like tone in her voice as she calmly pressed Jodi.

"I don't think you're the type of person that can sit there during your trial and see Travis' family sitting over there and continue to maintain that lie in yourself without it tearing you up," she said.

"I don't think I could either," Jodi replied.

Blaney continued to pry, but gently, with the focus on Jodi's character, not the heinous killing.

"You're not our typical suspect. You come from a good home, you're a bright girl. There's no question in my mind or any of the other investigators' minds that you were the person that took Travis' life. But what I need to know or what I'd like to know is . . . whether you're a cold-blooded, cold-hearted murderer who slaughtered this guy or are you somebody that got caught up in circumstances and things got out of control. Because I think that's what happened honestly."

It was stellar detective work on the part of Blaney. She was warming up the suspect, trying to get Jodi to open up. But really, Blaney just wanted her to confess and make it easier to lock her up for the rest of her life.

"Anybody could be capable of harming another person. It's in our nature . . . most people suppress that," Blaney said. "What I generally see are the cold-hearted ruthless types. What I don't see very often, Jodi, are people like yourself that are intelligent and spiritual and caring and so I tend to believe that it was an . . . incidental circumstance if you will."

Jodi was more closed down than the previous day, barely saying anything in response to Blaney's kinder, gentler approach. She cried when Blaney mentioned Travis' family, and Jodi noted how fond her slain lover was of his brothers and sisters.

"I can only imagine that keeping all of this in is tearing you apart inside. It's not hard to tell that, you know. You have portrayed yourself as being very strong, but you can see it in your eyes, Jodi," Blaney said.

"I fall apart when people aren't looking," Jodi said.

"Just because I'm a cop doesn't mean that I don't care, you know, about humanity and people. I'm not sitting here judging you. I'm trying to help you out. Trying to give you a chance to make things right," she said.

She then offered a preview of the harsh reality that was to come with her headline-grabbing murder trial.

"When this goes to trial, the media's there. It's not kept a secret. Do you want to be out there like O.J. Simpson . . .? You know, nobody respected him afterwards, even though he maintained his innocence."

Blaney told Jodi that this would certainly be big news soon.

"Do you want to be portrayed as that cold-blooded, cold-hearted murderer because the media loves that?" Blaney told her.

Jodi responded in a soft voice: "You know of course I don't want to be portrayed as a cold-blooded murderer."

Blaney went on: "This is kind of a pause, you know, before things start getting heavy. This is an opportunity to help yourself out. When the jury looks at it, those are the things they are going to be mulling around in their mind when they decide what type of sentence to hand out or when they make a recommendation to the judge. Those are the sorts of things that turn a jury, and juries can sometimes be fickle, but I've never seen a case with so much concrete hard evidence."

Jodi still wouldn't admit to the killing, and in fact, most of her answers took a different tack as she talked about how she would be portrayed in the media. Jodi asked about what would happen to her possessions, including a camera and a couple hundred bucks in cash that she was carrying when arrested.

She asked about her journals and told Blaney where authorities could find them—in her fireproof safe. She broke down in tears as she told Blaney that she shot a wedding for a couple named Brian and Katie the weekend before and that their photos were still on her camera. She said she was happy with how the photos turned out as she worked her magic with editing software.

"That's the only thing they have to remember the day," Jodi said.

"I think you're not grasping the reality of the situation," Blaney said, "and hearing what your concerns are, you should be concerned for yourself right now."

They went back and forth for the next 20 minutes or so as Blaney's patience grew thinner with each lie and Jodi's behavior grew more bizarre. Blaney left the room for a few minutes, and Jodi responded by sitting down on the floor, cowering under the table.

Blaney returned and tried to put more pressure on Jodi, seeing her apparent fear as a chance to get her when she was at her weakest.

"I'm at the end of my rope," Blaney said, now changing her tactics. "And what I'm hearing is somebody who doesn't give a crap about what happened. I'm hearing somebody who is worried about money, your appearance, everything about you. I don't hear anything about Travis, unless you're specifically asked."

Blaney gave Jodi countless opportunities to unleash her self-defense claim, practically putting the words in her mouth as she attempted to get a confession. "Was he roughing you up and you just couldn't take it?" she suggested. "Was he being violent on his part?"

Jodi made some references to their relationship being rocky and how Travis was violent with her and left her bruised. But she didn't go into the kind of painstaking detail that she did during her trial as she brought out the claim that she killed Travis because he was violently abusive.

Jodi never folded. They relentlessly pursued a confession for two days, but she never admitted to the killing.

If Jodi's behavior in the interrogation room was notable for her flippant demeanor and evasiveness, her mother's interview with Flores after her daughter's arrest was torturous for its heartbreaking nature.

Every mother and father dreads the day that they have to take a call from a police officer or school official telling them that their child has done something wrong.

Whether it's shoplifting a candy bar from a convenience store, getting detention for mouthing off at school, or getting caught drinking, the calls are always painful.

Being told your daughter is a murderer is pure torture.

Sandy Arias' pain was so palpable during her interview by Flores that it's difficult to watch. The tears, the sobs, the questions of "how this possibly could have happened" were distressing.

Sandy described Jodi's problems, her relationship with Travis, her behavior in the month or so since he died. She admitted Jodi's friends would call her over the years and say that Jodi needed help, that she had mental issues. One day Jodi would be fine, the next day she would call her mother in tears. Her mother said Jodi had trust issues and was always paranoid.

"Why would she do something like that? Did she snap? How could she come back here and be normal?" Sandy Arias pondered.

Through tears, she told Flores that Jodi was a "very intelligent person," and cited the many books she read in her life. She admitted their relationship had never been great and that Jodi clearly had mental issues, along with some "fantasy in her head" that she had a rotten childhood.

But a murderer? No way. Sandy said she felt like she was "going to puke."

Flores tried to console the sobbing mother, but also explained to her how real the situation was.

"The evidence is pretty damning," he said. "I've never had this much evidence in a case before."

14

"NO JURY
IS GOING TO CONVICT ME"

*"'Why, I can smile and murder whiles I smile/And cry 'content'
to that which grieves my heart/And wet my cheeks with artificial
tears/And frame my face for all occasions."*
—William Shakespeare

In the months after her arrest, Jodi finally started talking. She had moved on from her contention that she was not with Travis when he was killed. Then came her second story:

Jodi heard a loud noise. She was startled. Travis was with her in his master bathroom.

Suddenly, two murderous, blood thirsty intruders dressed in black, wearing ski masks and gloves, barged into the bathroom.

The man and woman stabbed and slashed Travis with ferocious power, leaving him bleeding on the floor.

Jodi was overcome with fear.

They slashed and stabbed Travis as he lay on the floor still alive, bleeding profusely. "I can't feel my legs!" Travis screamed.

Jodi charged the female burglar, despite the fact that the woman was carrying a knife. The male burglar became enraged at Jodi, presumably for fighting with his accomplice.

They now had to decide whether to kill Jodi. They argued back and forth about it.

Finally, they put the barrel of a gun to Jodi's forehead. This was it, she thought. She was about to die execution-style in a ruthless home invasion.

The intruder pulled the trigger. Nothing. The gun didn't fire. Jodi grabbed her purse, sprinted downstairs, ran outside, and sped away.

She knew Travis was still alive, but she was in so much shock that she just got out of there. The killers didn't chase after her, and Jodi didn't call 911. She just left.

If the story sounds a little ridiculous, that's because it was. Jodi made it up. And she told the story to the world after her arrest, including friends, family and journalists with *48 Hours, Inside Edition,* and *The Arizona Republic.*

"No jury is going to convict me . . . because I'm innocent, and you can mark my words on that one: No jury will convict me," Jodi told *Inside Edition.*

The masked intruder scenario was one of the three stories Jodi would tell after killing Travis.

Faced with mounting evidence against her and major holes in the intruder tale, Jodi changed her tune again. It was two years after her arrest and now this: She did it, but it was self-defense.

As part of her new story, Jodi started leveling a series of accusations during against Travis that cast him as a quick-tempered, physically abusive, sexual deviant.

Authorities believed she made it all up, pulling it out of thin air when she realized it was her only out, the only way to possibly avoid being convicted of first-degree murder: Demonize Travis.

Jodi claimed Travis was a violent man who had beaten her on at least four occasions, once even choking her into unconsciousness. Her defense attorneys would later depict these attacks as the beginning of Jodi's spiral into erratic behavior not uncommon among abused women.

She went on to explain Travis' many perversions: She fell asleep on a chair in his bedroom one night and awoke to find Travis aggressively performing oral sex on her. Rape, her defense attorneys would later claim at trial.

She said other times he coerced her into tawdry acts, and on numerous occasions she caved to his desire for anal sex. He grabbed her butt once at a convenience store while waiting in line in front of a bunch of truckers to make a point that she was his girl. He asked her to find a spot in the forest near Yreka where she could dress up like Little Red Riding Hood and make an amateur porn film. He also once smacked her on her head with the back of his hand.

As her story went, it all reached a tipping point on the day she killed him. She was already tired of Travis' demeaning behavior, the name-calling, the beatings.

She said he attacked her one last time, and she fought for her life.

15

TRAVIS ALEXANDER: IN MEMORIAM

*"I can honestly say that I awake every single day happy.
I am motivated by it."*

—Travis Alexander

The death of Travis Alexander was an unbelievable nightmare to everyone who knew him—church members, Prepaid Legal associates, and family members.

At his memorial service in June 2008, his family and friends played a montage of photos from Travis' life from his childhood until his death.

The presentation opened with the following quote from Travis:

I'm a simple man really. Smart, successful smashing good looks, a real suitor. I love nature, helping the homeless, and cooking with my grandmother just to create memories.

The presentation included music from Neil Diamond's "Man of God," "We're going to be Friends" and "Over the Rainbow/

What a Wonderful World." There were tears and smiles in the audience as they looked at dozens of photos: family portraits with siblings; childhood images of him riding a motorcycle, pushing a lawnmower and fishing; his senior and prom pictures from high school; photos of him and friends at Halloween parties, his Mormon baptism and Prepaid Legal events.

There were also several photos of him with girlfriends and other women in his life. One person was noticeably missing.

He and Jodi photographed practically every aspect of their lives, hundreds of pictures from their trips and times together. But there was no image of Jodi in the montage.

Later another quote from Travis: "I can honestly say that I awake every single day happy. I am motivated by it. To make it a day better than the last. To go to bed better than I woke up and to do it all over again the next day. I feel as if it is the way to live. To have purpose, to have righteous desire to make this world a better place because you are in it."

His obituary ran in the Riverside Press-Enterprise on June 17 and 18. His family paid tribute to him with the following statement:

Travis lived each day as if it were his last, with many accomplishments, dreams, travels, and successes. He was an amazing individual who sought out to save the world with his positive influence, his motivational speaking and his writing. He was well on his way to making all his dreams a reality. Travis has touched so many lives and will continue in our hearts forever and always. We can never express the unbearable pain from this tragedy. We love him so much, and cherished every precious moment with him. We will miss his smile, the way he made us laugh and everything about him!

16

"THE PERSON
WHO DONE IT . . . SITS
IN COURT"

After about a month of jury selection, a panel was seated
that included seven men and eleven women.

In Arizona, the final 12 who would ultimately decide Jodi's
fate were chosen at the conclusion of closing arguments to be
sure the six alternates paid close attention, too. After all, this
case couldn't get more serious. Jodi was on trial for her life.

In early January—about four and a half years after Jodi
killed Travis—the trial of the year finally began.

Prosecutor Juan Martinez immediately launched into his
narrative, clearly ready to get the trial going after months of
hearings and legal wrangling over what evidence would ultimately be presented to jurors.

"This is not a case of whodunit," Martinez told jurors. "The
person who done it, the person who committed this killing sits
in court today, the defendant, Jodi Ann Arias."

He went on to describe the couple's steamy relationship and how Jodi was clearly more into Travis than he was into her, how she was in love with him and had described Travis as one of the greatest blessings in her life.

"And this love, well, she rewarded that love for Travis Alexander by sticking a knife in his chest. And . . . he's a good man . . . And with regard to being a good man, well, she slit his throat as a reward for being a good man," Martinez told the jury.

"And in terms of these blessings," he continued, "well, she knocked the blessings out of him by putting a bullet in his head."

Martinez then described how the two met and their stormy relationship. He eventually came to the events that led up to the killing, a brutal attack he said was at the hands of a scorned lover in a fit of jealous rage.

He detailed the stabbing, Travis' fight for his life, the slitting of his throat, and the gunshot to the head. And he explained how Travis suffered a painful death.

"Mr. Alexander did not die calmly."

It was now defense attorney Jennifer Willmott's turn to tell jurors an entirely different story, yet one that began in much the same way.

"Jodi Arias killed Travis Alexander," Willmott said. "There is no question about it. The million dollar question is what would have forced her to do it?"

Willmott then laid out the alternate scenario. Travis attacked Jodi in a rage. It was kill or be killed.

"Jodi had to make a choice," Willmott said. "She would either live or she would die."

The attorney explained how Travis abused Jodi, but she admittedly kept coming back for more because she loved him.

"In Jodi he found somebody who was easily manipulated and controlled, someone who would provide him with that secretive sexual relationship that he needed, while on the outside he can still pursue the appropriate Mormon woman."

She described for jurors the duality of Travis' life—that of an outwardly devout Mormon saving sex for marriage while simultaneously being a private pervert using Jodi as his personal sex toy. She detailed how he told friends and family Jodi was stalking him, but continued beckoning her to meet him for trysts.

Willmott then moved on to the crux of the case—premeditation—and explained how the time stamps on photographs taken by Jodi on the day of the killing did not bear out a calculated attack. Travis is alive in one photograph, then clearly injured, the attack already under way, in another just about a minute later.

"Now, that very brief moment of time, a minute, is not the result of premeditation. It is not the result of a planned attack."

The prosecutor objected. Sustained.

"The evidence will show that this is not the result . . ." Willmott argued.

Martinez objected again, cutting her off.

"Counsel approach," Judge Sherry Stephens said.

This would begin the never-ending series of objections and private bench conferences between the judge and attorneys, their voices each time drowned out by a recording of static to prevent them from being heard by jurors and spectators in the gallery.

These very first objections and private meetings would foreshadow the long months ahead, dragged out by one objection and one bench conference after another as the attorneys argued over the minutia of even individual words.

"The objection is she can't make the argument that this wasn't premeditated. That's just for closing arguments," Martinez told the judge.

"The evidence is going to show this wasn't premeditation," Willmott fired back. "I don't think I'm saying that the facts are going to show it wasn't planned."

"Argue the facts, OK, and the evidence, and don't talk about premeditation," Judge Stephens told her.

Willmott was confused.

"I just want to clarify. I think I can say that the evidence will show . . . that this is not premeditated," she said.

"I'll allow you to make that statement at the end," the judge replied. "Do you see what I'm saying? You can talk about specific facts you believe the evidence will show and talk about how they should interpret those facts."

"OK," Willmott replied before continuing her opening statement.

"In that one minute, had Jodi not chosen to defend herself, she would not be here."

The trial would continue for more than four months in downtown Phoenix at the Maricopa County Courthouse as it snowballed into one of the most watched and talked about cases of a generation.

17

#JODIARIAS

"They're selling postcards of the hanging.
They're painting the passports brown.
The beauty parlor is filled with sailors.
The circus is in town."

—Bob Dylan

Even Jodi had a Twitter account.

The defendant on trial for her life made a series of Twitter posts, at times even waxing poetic, in a testament to the influence of social media on the case.

"We own nothing but the talents God have given to us to improve upon, to show Him what we will do with them," Jodi posted in one Tweet from early April, citing the words of Brigham Young.

She took subtle jabs at the prosecutor, posting: "Hmm . . . Anger Management problems anyone?"

"HLN is an acronym for Haters Love Negativity," she railed in another post, referencing Turner Broadcasting's cable network, where Nancy Grace and other shows covered the trial practically nonstop day and night.

A woman in the gallery claimed to be tweeting on Jodi's behalf, gathering the comments from her during jail phone calls. "She'll call and say, 'I have a quote.' We'll talk about it. Sometimes she says 'Let's tweet.' And then she'll say 'No let's not do it,'" Donavan Bering told Fox affiliate KSAZ in Phoenix.

"I think it's a way of her getting out her frustration, because she doesn't have a chance to say much," said Donavan.

Jodi gathered nearly 35,000 followers.

Meanwhile, she was hawking her artwork drawn with colored pencils from jail, some pieces, according to her website, fetching more than $1,200. The site, www.jodiarias.com, was being operated by a third party, selling the items such as a drawing of Frank Sinatra for $1,075, and another offered for $2,000. Shipping was included.

Her mother told the *Associated Press* during the trial that the money was being used to help pay for the family's expenses while attending the proceedings each day for more than four months.

Jodi's behavior encapsulated the tone of the circus that would envelop the proceedings from start to finish.

This trial, after all, was as much about the case as it was about the times. The era of cameras in the courtroom had come of age during O.J. Simpson but this time it would be streamed live via the Internet, carrying the entirety of each day's events unedited to viewers around the world.

Interest soared with each day of testimony as the public became virtual participants with their own interactions through Facebook, Twitter and any number of websites, including Wild About Trial, whose reporter in the courtroom spent hours on end conversing with enthusiasts.

The year-old company epitomized the changing climate in which the public wanted to consume information about such salacious cases. They no longer seemed satisfied with sound bites on the evening news. They wanted to watch every second. They wanted to interact. They wanted to be part of the action.

Entire online communities revolved around the trial. There was a Facebook page called Justice4Travis that posted all things inflammatory about Jodi, and some really nasty comments. The page had more than 41,000 likes.

Then there was www.Jodiisinnocent.com that advertised itself as "The #1 Jodi Arias Support Site."

The Twitter page @KirkNumri was set up to mock the defense attorney dressed daily in loosely fitting suits that hung from his large frame like drapes. Sites emerged about prosecutor Juan Martinez, too, some attacking him, some heaping praise.

The Arizona Republic reported that defense attorney Jennifer Willmott had received death threats, but declined to pursue police investigations.

A transcript of one voicemail left for the lawyer was provided to the newspaper during the trial:

"You don't have to return my call, but I'm just telling you: If Jodi, if you get her off of the death penalty, we will find you, we know where you're at, we will kill you," the caller said.

The newspaper also reported that psychotherapist Alyce LaViolette, a defense expert witness who testified that Jodi suffered from battered woman's syndrome, was being attacked in phone calls, emails, and over the Internet by people fuming over her support for Jodi.

The absurdities would continue even inside the courtroom, where one day testimony turned to the tale of Snow White. LaViolette once gave a seminar called "Was Snow White a Battered Woman?" and Martinez ripped her credibility for it.

The prosecutor questioned her loudly about how she came

to the conclusion that Snow White was abused, to which the defense witness replied that he was mischaracterizing her presentation.

The questioning and testimony only grew more bizarre as the hours passed.

Martinez explained how Snow White was banished to the forest to live in horrible conditions.

"She lived with the seven dwarves and according to the Disney version, she was pretty happy," LaViolette said.

"She lived in a shack, right?" Martinez snapped loudly.

"I thought it was a cute little cabin, Mr. Martinez," LaViolette replied.

"Mr. Martinez, are you angry at me?" LaViolette asked softly at one point. Portions of the gallery erupted in laughter, and the judge admonished spectators to keep quiet.

"Do you want to spar with me?" Martinez yelled, continuing to question her about whether Snow White was a domestic abuse victim.

"I have no information about the relationship between Prince Charming and Snow White," LaViolette said.

The two sparred for days as LaViolette bobbed and weaved around Martinez's questions.

At one point, LaViolette, who counsels domestic abuse victims and abusers, lashed out at Martinez as he raised his voice.

"If you were in my group, I would ask you to take a time out, Mr. Martinez," she said.

Outside court, Jodi's trial became like a live daytime soap opera. But for many, that wasn't good enough. They had to be there.

Dozens of people flocked to court each day, lining up in the early morning hours for a chance to score one of a handful of seats open to the public. The seats were provided on a first-come, first-served basis, and as the trial dragged on, the crowds only grew.

One week toward the end of testimony, a trial regular sold her spot in line to another person for $200. Both were reprimanded by court officials. The money was returned, but the purchaser got to keep her seat in the courtroom.

While there is no specific law preventing the public from selling their spot in line to get into the trial, Phoenix criminal defense lawyer Julio Laboy said it undermined the seriousness of the case.

"People lose sight of how very real this is," Laboy told the AP, noting it was a case about a violent killing that could send one person to death row. "It's extremely disheartening, as if people were bartering to get into a Yankees game."

The sideshow of the Arias trial was evident everywhere, even on the courthouse steps, where spectators would gather daily for a chance to catch a glimpse of the star of the show—Martinez.

At one point, as several dozen trial fans gathered outside the courthouse, they were elated when Martinez emerged. He typically took another exit, and would never use the front door again, but seemed blown away by his growing number of fans, clearly caught off-guard.

Kathy Brown, 49, approached him and had him autograph her cane.

"I just love watching him," she said. "I love the passion he has."

The antics would later lead to a charge by the defense of prosecutorial misconduct. Two HLN staffers were even questioned in open court about what they had witnessed during the odd episode that seemed more befitting of a Hollywood red carpet event than a murder trial. The judge wanted to know if any jurors had seen the gaggle gathered around Martinez.

The trial moved on, and the social media world continued to blow up with all things Jodi.

Twitter became such a driving force behind the immense interest in the case that even the hometown newspaper, *The Arizona Republic*, didn't publish stories every day of the trial. Instead, the paper's regular trial reporter, a seasoned newsman named Michael Kiefer—@michaelbkiefer—spent many days just tweeting the minutiae of every turn in the case, communicating the daily happenings in real time with his growing number of followers around the world.

By this time, just about every television network had at least one reporter or producer in the courtroom. ABC's *Good Morning America* covered the trial on a regular basis and even broke news, obtaining hundreds of pages from Jodi's diary as the proceedings were ongoing.

NBC's *Dateline* was there. So was CBS' *48 Hours*. CNN aired almost nightly programs for a time, and HLN saw its ratings soar.

HLN programs hosted by Nancy Grace, Jane Velez-Mitchell, and Dr. Drew Pinsky were all averaging nearly 700,000 daily viewers in April, with most of them tuning in to get updated on Jodi's case. For Velez-Mitchell and Dr. Drew, their numbers were about double the ratings from the previous April. HLN's daytime programs did exceptionally well, too, topping MSNBC among the key 25- to 54-year-old demographic.

HLN brought in ordinary Americans to fill out mock juries who decided various elements of the case. The network would go on to produce a dramatized re-enactment of the events that could have occurred in Travis' bathroom the day Jodi says he attacked her, body-slammed her to the tile floor, and forced her to fight for her life.

A law enforcement expert played the role of Travis in front

of a mannequin that was supposed to be Jodi. He picked up the figure and slammed it to the floor.

The station then turned to the expertise of professional wrestler David Otunga.

Yes, a professional wrestler was now providing expert commentary on a capital murder case.

"If you got slammed on a tile floor, you're going to be incapacitated, definitely," Otunga explained. "I mean, it hurts when we get slammed in the ring, but just on a floor with no mat, no padding. That's going to be it."

Not that Jodi could have watched the coverage on TV when she went back to her jail cell every night. She was housed at the Estrella Jail for women in Phoenix, where inmates dine on a stew-like concoction along with mashed potatoes, vegetables and bread—and they don't have Internet access. Their TV selection before lights-out at 10 p.m. does not include HLN.

Adding to the increasing drama surrounding the case, three jurors were removed in the waning weeks of testimony.

Juror No. 5, a woman, was dismissed April 2, reportedly for making statements that showed bias. Just two days later, however, the woman returned to the courtroom as a spectator, stunning everyone in the gallery, including reporters, who later chased after her as she was led out a secret exit by a deputy.

Two other jurors were later excused, one for health reasons and the other because he was arrested on a DUI charge.

As if all the antics inside and outside the courtroom weren't enough, Jodi was always there to provide more fodder to fuel the fire.

Video was released of Jodi singing during an *American Idol*-style competition while she was being jailed in 2010 awaiting trial.

The jail system here is run by Sheriff Joe Arpaio, the self-described "Toughest Sheriff in America" who made a name for himself with his trademark and controversial hard-line approach to illegal immigration and gimmicks like making inmates wear pink underwear and work on chain gangs.

But Arpaio also shows a soft side each year with the inmate singing contest over the holidays.

Dressed in a striped jail outfit, Jodi belted out a sweet, unaccompanied version of the Christmas classic "O Holy Night" Sheriff Joe sat at the judging table a few feet away, next to a man dressed up as Santa Claus.

Jodi was up against men and women of all races, including an Elvis impersonator who led the inmates in a version of "Blue Christmas."

When the performances were finished, the judges rendered their verdict: Jodi was the winner.

A night divine, indeed, just as the song she sang. The prize was a holiday feast for Jodi and her fellow inmates—turkey and all the fixings, cranberries, you name it.

"I appreciate your vote. Thank you very, very much," Jodi told the crowd of prisoners. "I don't have much I can give right now and it means a lot to me."

18

THE BULLDOG

"Can you imagine how much it must have hurt Mr. Alexander when you stuck that knife right into his chest?"

—Juan Martinez

Maricopa County prosecutor Juan Martinez is a small man with a loud voice and an angry demeanor when he is ferociously questioning adversaries—sometimes even his own witnesses.

Outside court, he's cordial and gregarious, and attracted a fan following who flocked to the courthouse each day for a chance to catch a glimpse of the man who hoped to see Jodi Arias join just two other women on Arizona's death row.

He's done it before.

Known as a bulldog with a never-let-up approach to prosecuting cases and questioning witnesses, Martinez won a first-degree murder conviction in 2005 against Wendi Andrianoin, who was about the same age as Jodi when she poisoned, bludgeoned, and stabbed her husband to death in the couple's Phoenix-area home.

Much like Jodi, Andriano also testified in her own defense during her four-month trial, claiming she had been battered by her husband, and on the day he died, he flew into a rage and she was forced to defend herself.

Martinez, who has been a county prosecutor for 25 years, the last 17 solely focused on homicide cases, portrayed Andriano as a greedy, cheating wife who savagely killed her ailing husband.

The jury took just four hours to find the killing so especially cruel that it merited consideration for the ultimate punishment. Then, in just four days of deliberations after hearing testimony in the penalty phase, the panel returned a recommendation that she be put to death.

Martinez emerged victorious.

During Jodi's trial, Martinez was at it again. Ferocious. Unstoppable. Unapologetically intimidating.

He shuffled across the courtroom floor, rarely staying at the podium or even in one spot too long. He snapped at witnesses after rapid-fire questions, followed simply by him saying, "Yes or no." He raised his voice in anger when witnesses meandered, and objected at every turn.

Martinez became the star, unusual in such high-profile cases.

It's typically the flamboyant defense attorneys who gain notoriety as they work to get their client off and bask in the spotlight of all the publicity.

But defense attorneys Kirk Nurmi and Jennifer Willmott would largely remain a backdrop to Martinez's dramatic performance. Nurmi, a tall, burly man with a crew cut, beard and a serious demeanor in questioning witnesses, stood in sharp contrast to Willmott, much more casual and gregarious in her approach. Nurmi was given the more uncomfortable assignments, quizzing Jodi and other women about their sex lives in a bid to discredit Travis.

While Martinez was clearly the main attraction, the trial transformed Nurmi, Willmott and Judge Sherry Stephens into national figures as well.

Stephens has been presiding over cases in the Phoenix area for more than a decade, following more than 20 years as a prosecutor for the Arizona Attorney General.

The judge provided much leeway to lawyers throughout the case, largely because it was a death penalty trial, and she wanted to cover her bases. She kept a rigid schedule, often starting her day handling other cases on her docket.

Jodi's trial typically began at 10 a.m., followed by an hour and a half lunch break, and then an afternoon session that ended at 4:30 p.m. Jurors also got one 15-minute break every day.

Stephens also ended up with a larger role than most judges because of Arizona law that allows jurors to question witnesses as a matter of rule. Stephens read each question aloud to witnesses, often in a monotone voice that resembled the tone of a schoolteacher. She would tilt her head down, her glasses resting toward the tip of her nose, as she ticked off one question after another in a detached demeanor.

Nurmi and Willmott had been assigned the case. Jodi couldn't afford a private lawyer, so Arizona taxpayers would pick up the tab. The longer the trial went on, the more the public outrage grew as the price tag to taxpayers ballooned. It is a right afforded to all citizens, but it is does not come cheaply when you are dealing with a trial that lasts more than four months and requires years of pretrial motions and arguments.

By the end of the trial, the cost of Jodi's defense exceeded $1.7 million.

19

THE PROSECUTION

"I did not kill Travis."

—Jodi Arias

The state called Detective Flores to the stand.

Flores, the lead investigator, ambled to the witness stand and took jurors through the bizarre beginning, not just the discovery of Alexander's body, but the telephone calls he received from Jodi.

Jodi wanted to help. Anything the detective needed. Jodi was there for him. "Who could have done this?" she pondered. It was unimaginable. The detective, too, found it unimaginable. And after a while, unbelievable.

It was June 10, 2008, a day after Travis' body was found.

Jodi called Flores and explained how she hadn't seen her one-time boyfriend in about two months.

"I heard that he passed away, and that, I don't know, I heard all kinds of rumors," she said on the recorded call played for jurors in court.

Jurors heard Jodi tell Flores she moved back to California in April, and that was the last time she saw Travis after their relationship ended.

"You haven't come back in town since then?" Flores asked.

"No, I haven't," Jodi replied on the call.

She then explained how she knew of no enemies Travis had, and no weapons he kept in the home.

Flores knew something wasn't right. After all, Travis' friends immediately fingered Jodi as the possible culprit. The odds were clearly stacked against her.

As in so many criminal cases, the lies always come back to haunt the suspect. Jodi's challenges would be formidable as the prosecution made quick work of its part in less than two weeks. The case seemed clear, the evidence irrefutable.

Martinez pointed out how Jodi's palm print was found in blood at the scene, along with the nude photos of her and Travis time-stamped on the day he died.

Then there was the gun, and the unbelievable coincidence of the same caliber pistol being stolen from Jodi's grandparents also being used to shoot Travis in the forehead.

All of this, combined with the sheer brutality of the attack, the rage with which it was carried out, not just a single gunshot or a few stab wounds, but a virtual butchering of Travis' body, would prove formidable obstacles for Jodi's defense.

"Her changing stories, the confession, the forensic evidence, it's just a very difficult case to defend," California criminal defense lawyer Mark Geragos told *The Associated Press* at the time.

The defense's only hope was to spare Jodi the death penalty using expert witness after expert witness to show what a perverted letch Travis was, how he abused her, how her entire life was a series of wrong turns and dead ends, trying to gain sympathy from the jury. Her biggest problem would be the lies.

Martinez proceeded to call numerous witnesses, portraying Jodi as a cold-hearted killer who took Travis' life with so little emotion and afterthought that she went to see another man a day later for an intimate encounter.

Ryan Burns was called to the witness stand. He explained how he met Jodi at a Prepaid Legal convention in Oklahoma in April 2008. They exchanged numbers and within a few weeks began chatting on the phone often.

Toward the end of May 2008, just weeks before Jodi would kill Travis, Burns told jurors Jodi made plans to come visit him in Utah.

She arrived on June 4, 2008, explaining that she was late because she had gotten lost and needed to stop to rest. But something immediately struck Burns, he would testify.

Jodi had cuts on her hands.

"She had two small bandages on a couple of her fingers," Burns told jurors. Jodi explained she had cut herself on broken glass while working in a restaurant.

Little did Burns know, the woman he would later spend the night with had just savagely attacked and killed her last boyfriend. Burns said the two watched a movie at his home in West Jordan, Utah, just outside Salt Lake City.

He said things soon got heated as they grew intimate.

"We were talking and we kissed . . . Every time we started kissing it got a little more escalated," Burns testified.

"Eventually, we stopped," said Burns, also a devout Mormon. "I didn't want to go any further."

Later that night the couple attended a Prepaid legal event then joined others at a nearby restaurant.

"She was fine, she was laughing about simple little things like any other person. I never once felt like anything was wrong during the day," Burns told jurors.

After dinner, the two went back to Burns' home and napped. When they awoke, things again heated up.

"She got on top of me pretty aggressively and we were kissing. She was right on top of me," Burns said, explaining how the encounter soon cooled down just like earlier in the day.

He told jurors Jodi left his home at about 1 a.m. to head back to California.

After his testimony, Burns appeared on HLN for an interview with Nancy Grace, explaining how "very awkward" the entire saga has been.

"It's hard to believe you're this close to something so dramatic," Burns said. "I really didn't think she could have possibly done it."

Burns went on to describe how he spoke with Jodi on the phone just hours after she had killed Travis while she headed to Utah to see him.

"For that whole hour," he told Grace, "we talked about simple things, giggling about just little jokes, just like normal conversation you would think, obviously very abnormal in retrospect.

"She seemed just like the Jodi that I'd been talking to for five or six weeks the entire 14 hours that she was with me the day after Travis died."

Jodi's lies, and the stories she weaved in the days and months after killing Travis, were becoming the crux of the prosecution's case against her. These weren't the actions of a woman who had just killed a man in self-defense, the prosecutor explained.

This woman was a murderer, clear and simple.

Jurors would later hear from Maricopa County Medical Examiner Dr. Kevin Horn, who explained the severity of Travis' wounds and the ferociousness of the attack.

Horn described gashes on Travis' hands and feet, clearly defensive wounds as he tried to fight off his attacker, and how it was extremely unlikely that Travis would have been able to do much at all after the gunshot wound to the head. This testimony clearly contradicted Jodi's story that she shot him first but he kept coming after her, knocking the gun from her hand and forcing her to resort to the stabbing to save her own life.

Jurors heard a phone message Jodi left Travis just hours after the killing as she began to meticulously plan her alibi to avoid suspicion and cover her tracks.

"My phone died so I wasn't able to get back to anybody," Jodi explained on the call, adding that she wouldn't be able to make it to Travis' home for a visit on her road trip.

Jurors also were repeatedly reminded of her lies to Flores and others upon her arrest in California just about a month after the killing.

She sobbed as police questioned her, but stuck to her story that she wasn't involved—even after being shown the pictures that put her at the scene on the day he died.

The July 15, 2008 videotaped interrogation was played for jurors as Detective Flores grilled the defendant, explaining that all the evidence pointed to her involvement. She insisted she didn't kill him.

"You shot him in the head, then you got a knife and you stabbed him," Flores told her. "Jodi, tell me the truth, please."

"I did not kill Travis," Jodi replied.

Then she said something odd, something that puzzled even the veteran police detective.

She explained that if she were to have killed him, she couldn't have stabbed him. It would have been too cruel.

"I don't think I could stab him. I think I would have to shoot him until he was dead if that were my intentions," Jodi told the detective. "If I had it in me to kill him, the least I could have done was make it as humane as possible."

Flores confronted Jodi with the photographs, specifically an unintentional shot of Jodi's leg and a portion of Travis' bloodied body.

"It's your foot, Jodi. These are your pants," Flores told her.

"This is his bathroom. That is not my foot," Jodi replied.

And she continued with the lies even though at this point, police had everything they needed to prove Jodi was there when Travis died, even that Jodi must have been the one who killed him.

Martinez showed jurors the gruesome photos of Travis' bloated body, and pictures taken by police at his home of her handprint and footprints in blood.

Jodi sat at the defense table, visibly shaken by the reality of what was occurring. She couldn't bear to look at the pictures. She covered her face. She looked away. It was just too much for her to relive.

She had a similar reaction when the infamous phone sex recording from May 2008 was played for the jury.

Jodi's defense attorneys were preparing to portray her as a love-struck emotional basket case who only begrudgingly agreed to participate in so many raunchy sex acts to please Travis, to make him happy, and to calm his constant rage toward her.

Martinez was clearly working to paint a picture of a woman who was as much into the sex as Travis was, even instigating it often, introducing lubricant into their relationship as Jodi complained the anal sex grew painful.

He displayed text messages between Jodi and Travis exchanged about three months before his death.

"Maybe u could give my ass a much-needed pounding," Jodi wrote. "I want to fuck you like a dirty, horny little school girl."

The case against her grew stronger with every day of testimony, every raunchy photograph, every recording and text message, and every lie Jodi told police, friends and family before eventually settling on self-defense.

The prosecution's final witness before resting its case on January17, 2013, was a female friend of Jodi who had dinner with her 24 hours after Travis was killed.

"She was acting like Jodi, the same Jodi I always talk to," Leslie Udy testified, adding she had been friends with Jodi for about two years at that time.

Udy told jurors she had a long talk that night with Jodi, who called Travis her best friend.

"She said that they weren't together anymore, which I kind of already knew," Udy said.

But Jodi told her she and Travis would "always be friends."

Days later, Udy said Jodi called her in tears to tell her the news of Travis' death. Jodi acted shocked. Distraught. Confused. Again, she pondered, who could have done this?

"She couldn't imagine why someone could do something like that to Travis, that he was such a wonderful person and why would anybody do that to him," Udy told jurors.

Martinez was done—for now. His point was made. Jodi is a liar. She lied from the start, and was still lying now.

20

THE BODY

"CAUSE OF DEATH: Sharp force trauma of neck and torso.
MANNER: Homicide."
—Autopsy report for Travis Alexander

Travis' body was a mess. His brain had turned to mush after about five days decomposing in his shower.

The Maricopa County Medical Examiner's report would describe the wounds in precise detail. During the trial, Martinez showed the photos of Travis' mutilated corpse over and over to jurors, emphasizing the sheer brutality of the attack Jodi delivered upon him. He needed the jury to see the wounds, to imagine what it would have been like to suffer such trauma, such pain, such anguish as the life left his body.

Travis' family sobbed and looked away. Jodi, too, couldn't bear to see the pictures. Each time they were displayed on a large screen in the courtroom, she looked down, also sobbing.

Stab wounds to the head, to the neck, chest, stomach, shoulders, back, and feet, nearly 30 in all, including five on his hands, presumably as he fought furiously to defend himself. He also had a single gunshot wound above his right eyebrow.

His throat had been slit from ear to ear.

Jodi claimed she shot Travis first, but he didn't die, and kept coming after her, forcing her to fend him off with the knife. While she couldn't recall actually stabbing him, blaming her memory loss on the trauma of the attack, she conceded she must have done it.

Part of the prosecution case would come down to the order in which the attack occurred. Prosecutors said it was clear she stabbed him first repeatedly in a blitz assault, and after he was likely already dead, she then shot him in the head. They needed to convince the jury that the killing happened in this order, since it would clearly counter her self-defense claim.

Why would she need to shoot him after he was no longer a threat, after he was bleeding all over and near death, if not already dead?

It was a crucial fact in the case that prosecutors needed to prove in order to help secure a first-degree murder conviction and the death penalty.

Dr. Kevin Horn, who performed the autopsy, testified the gunshot wound would have likely rendered Travis unconscious and unable to defend himself.

"Again because of the injury to the brain, the information processing part of the brain would have rendered him unable to raise his hands to offer any sort of purposeful action or to verbalize anything," Horn said.

Horn's testimony would be a tough obstacle for the defense to overcome, as he said there was no way Travis could have continued to fight after being shot in the head, as Jodi claimed.

"If the bullet wound was the first wound that was received

by Mr. Alexander, would it have been immediately incapacitating?" Martinez asked him.

"Yes," Horn replied.

"And why would it have been incapacitating?" Martinez continued.

"Because of brain injury," Horn said.

A juror query for Horn would sum up his testimony, and obviously later send the panel into deliberations with some serious questions.

"Can you explain why you think Travis was still alive when his throat was cut?"

"Because of the large amount of hemorrhage into the soft tissue around the throat wound," Horn replied. "That requires a beating heart."

21

THE DEFENSE

"They're probably watching me. Well, let them.
Let them see what kind of a person I am. I'm not even going to swat
that fly. . . . They'll see and they'll know, and they'll say,
"Why, she wouldn't even harm a fly."

—*Psycho*

Jodi's defense attorneys began presenting their case January 29, 2013. It went on for nearly two and a half months, delving deep into Jodi's life, with witness after witness describing her as a gentle soul, an unassuming woman who was in search of herself.

Their task was daunting. Here is a defendant who had admitted to lying, to creating an alibi to avoid suspicion and arrest, who lied repeatedly about her involvement, who fled the scene of the killing without calling police and without ever checking to see if Travis could be saved.

The self-defense claim, too, would be an enormous challenge. At the heart of it all was convincing jurors that Travis was a violent man, an abusive womanizer who had attacked Jodi at least four times in the past, kicking her in the ribs, breaking her finger and once even choking her into unconsciousness.

The problem was that no evidence or testimony supported

her claims. She never called police to report the abuse. She never took photographs to document her injuries—something one would think an aspiring photographer would do without even thinking about it. And she never even wrote about any of the abuse in her detailed diaries.

She would later explain it was because of her belief in the law of attraction, a notion made popular by the movie, *The Secret*. The idea was simple—only put out to the world the sort of energy you want in return. Talking, writing or even thinking negatively only begets more negativity. Jodi insisted she lived by this rule.

But the lack of documentation of Travis' abuse would haunt the defense. Their only hope was to portray Jodi as the victim, Travis as the perpetrator.

Their case would rest largely on demonizing Travis and portraying him as a liar and a cheat who used Jodi to fulfill his raunchy fantasies, berated her publicly and privately, beat her when things didn't go his way, and ultimately, tried to attack her one last time on the day of his death.

The defense tactic throughout the case was clear—introduce the jury to Jodi, give them the opportunity to get to know her, through multiple witnesses and eventually, through her own words during 18 days on the witness stand.

It was not an unsurprising approach. The case against Jodi was damning. At the very least, defense attorneys hoped that if the jury did convict her of first-degree murder, they would spare her life after coming to know the gentle person she was deep inside.

And with that, the case went into slow motion, and continued that way for weeks, one day dragging into another as reporters and spectators grew bored with the seemingly never-ending tale of Jodi's life.

The first defense witness talked mostly about his business mentoring relationship with Jodi through Prepaid Legal, and described her as feminine but conservative.

Next up was ex-boyfriend Daryl Brewer, who told jurors how Jodi had become more involved with the Mormon church after meeting Travis. Brewer also explained that he never saw Jodi become violent or jealous toward other women in his life. But he described her as sexually aggressive—something that did not work in the defense favor—and said she once took a nude picture of him in the shower.

An ex-girlfriend of Travis later testified that he cheated on her with Jodi and lied to her about being a virgin, which played right into the defense case that Travis was just out for sex. However, the same woman said Travis had never been physically or emotionally abusive to her.

Another friend of Travis told jurors about their involvement in the Mormon faith, and again repeated claims that Travis had portrayed himself to be a virgin.

Another dilemma for the defense was the gun—the very weapon Jodi acknowledged disposing of somewhere in the desert as she fled the scene of the killing, and the very same caliber used to shoot Travis.

How could it be such a coincidence that Travis was shot with a .25 caliber pistol, and the same caliber was stolen from the Northern California home of Jodi's grandparents—where she had been staying—just a week before the killing?

The defense never even tried to explain away the gun. Jodi simply denied that she took it, and insisted that she shot Travis with his own gun that he kept in his closet—coincidentally, a .25 caliber pistol. But again, there was a problem. There was no evidence, no spare bullets, no holster, no gun box, nothing at Travis' home to prove he ever even owned the weapon.

And no one testified throughout the trial that Travis owned a gun. No one. Not a shred of evidence. But the defense stuck with this story.

At the time, pundits, trial watchers, and lawyers following the case everywhere thought surely the defense would have a better explanation. Nancy Grace railed about the case every night, condemning Jodi as a murderer.

Jodi had admitted to lying so many times in the past, blaming it on fear and shame, that one more lie couldn't have made a difference. She could have easily acknowledged she took the gun, if only for self-defense against a man she claimed had been abusing her. But she didn't.

The story of Jodi's entire defense would largely rest on her words, her accounts, her assertions. Sure, the text messages, the phone recordings, the emails, all showed that Travis was clearly not the man he presented himself to be publicly. He was a Mormon. He was looking for a good wife of faith, but he also liked having sex with Jodi. There was just no question about it. Travis' own words proved it.

But just who was the sexual aggressor in the relationship always remained unclear.

And for the jury to make the leap to self-defense, they would have to believe that not only was Travis very much into sex with as many women as he could get into bed—and some pretty kinky sex at that—but that he was a physically violent man toward women. None of his past girlfriends or acquaintances described him as such a person.

A defense expert testified that Jodi suffered from post-traumatic stress disorder and amnesia, explaining why Jodi couldn't recall much from the day she killed Travis.

Another expert told jurors Jodi was indeed abused by Travis and suffered from battered woman's syndrome. Enter the prosecution expert who later countered it all, saying Jodi suffered from none of the diagnoses and instead had borderline personality disorder, a severe mental illness marked by unstable moods in behavior and relationships that can lead to brief psychotic episodes.

These dueling expert witnesses would become crucial to the defense case aimed at saving Jodi's life.

But the key to it all was for jurors to hear directly from Jodi herself. In many death penalty trials, the defendant never takes the stand. It creates too many chances for an aggressive prosecutor to poke holes in their stories, and catch the person off guard, creating a *Perry Mason*-style gotcha moment that could clinch the case for a conviction.

In the U.S. justice system, defendants are innocent until proven guilty, meaning it's not the job of defense attorneys to prove their client didn't commit the crime. Prosecutors must prove that they did.

Defense lawyers merely have to create enough confusion in the prosecution case to raise reasonable doubt.

And that's exactly what Jodi had hoped to do for herself.

22

JODI TAKES THE STAND

"**M**s. Arias, you may come forward and take a seat, please," the judge said to stunned whispers in the gallery.

Jodi got up from the defense table and walked gingerly across the courtroom to the witness stand. She was dressed in a black shirt and khaki pants. Her stringy bangs were combed straight down over her forehead, almost touching her glasses. She looked homely. Bland. Childish. Innocent.

In their haste to get her to the stand before the jury entered the room, court officials forgot to swear her in. Defense attorneys had requested she be seated before the panel was present so jurors couldn't see her electronic ankle bracelet placed on her by authorities each time she left jail for trial.

Now the formality.

"The defense calls Jodi Arias," said her attorney, Kirk Nurmi.

Jodi stood and raised her right hand to be sworn in, then sat again. The jury was now in the room.

"Hi Jodi," Nurmi said in a gentle voice, as if speaking to someone at a funeral.

"Hi," she replied, a smirk appearing for just a split second before her lips shrank back into an emotionless line across her face.

"How are you feeling right now?" Nurmi asked.

"Um, nervous," Jodi said, shifting around in her chair.

"Is this a position you ever thought you would find yourself in, testifying here today?"

Martinez objected. Relevance. Attorneys approached the bench to argue with the judge privately. Jodi's mother sat in the gallery stone-faced. Travis' family watched from the front row just across the room.

Nurmi moved on to another line of questioning.

"Let me ask you a couple of important questions before we get back and start talking about who you are and why you're here, OK?" he said.

Jodi nodded. "OK."

"Did you kill Travis Alexander on June 4, 2008?" Nurmi asked slowly, practically stopping after each word.

Jodi swiveled in her chairand looked to the jury.

"Yes, I did," she said

"Why?" Nurmi prodded.

"Um," Jodi started, again turning her chair to face the jury. "The simple answer is that he attacked me."

She paused.

"And I defended myself," Jodi continued.

Nurmi wanted to get some of the most problematic things out first before he spent the ensuing days questioning Jodi about the minutia of her entire life, from childhood to now.

He asked her about the interview she did for *Inside Edition* after being arrested and charged in Travis' death. At the time, she was sticking to the story of the intruders, though it wouldn't be long before she changed the tale once more.

"I understand all the evidence is really compelling," Jodi said in the TV interview. "In a nutshell, two people came in and killed Travis. I've never even shot a gun. That's heinous. I can't imagine slitting anyone's throat."

Then came the kicker.

"No jury will convict me and you can mark my words on that," Jodi told *Inside Edition*. "I'm innocent."

Nurmi asked her if she remembered saying that.

"Yeah, I did say that," Jodi replied.

"Why?"

"At the time, I had plans to commit suicide," Jodi said.

She paused to sigh, rubbing her hands on her legs nervously as her gaze dropped down. She lifted her head and looked to the jury again.

"I was extremely confident that no jury would convict me because I didn't expect any of you to be here," she told the panel.

"I didn't expect to be here, so I could have very easily have said no jury would acquit me either," she continued, explaining that she couldn't tell the interviewer for the TV show that she was going to commit suicide because a jail guard was nearby.

"I would have been thrown into a padded cell, stripped down and that would have been my life for a while until I stabilized," she said. "So I was very confident that no jury would convict me because I planned to be dead."

Jodi went on for more than a week recounting in precise detail one life event after another—from a troubled childhood marred by abuse at the hands of her parents, a string of bad relationships, and how Travis belittled her, cheated on her, called her derogatory names like whore, skank, and "three-hole wonder," and used her to fulfill his sexual fantasies.

She explained that she continued to see Travis for sex even after they broke up and she learned he had been cheating on her because she had low "self-esteem."

"I was kind of a doormat," Jodi said, staring sheepishly at jurors, a pure look of innocence in her eyes.

She explained how Travis once beat her, pushed her to the ground, kicked her in the ribs and broke her finger, then in a theatrical moment for the jury, raised her hand to display her crooked digit. She later detailed three more accounts of abuse at the hands of Travis.

She told jurors she never sought medical treatment because she was worried authorities would get involved, and that Travis' name would be sullied. She said she was later ashamed of herself.

"I used to think that women in situations like that, that it was partially, if not equally, their fault because they kept staying there," Jodi said.

"Great, now I'm one of those people," she told jurors she thought to herself.

Her testimony was aimed at setting up the defense expert who would explain the realities of battered woman's syndrome, how they rarely report the abuse and feel as if the violence against them was a result of their own actions.

Jodi then continued to detail Travis' perversions as she described how she once awoke from sleeping in his bed to find him having sex with her, an incident for which she felt responsible.

"I went to sleep next to him. I was wearing a T-shirt, cute shorts," Jodi said, repeating over and over how Travis made her feel like a prostitute, and how she fulfilled his fantasies, including wearing boy's underwear and having sex with him in public.

She also told jurors how she once walked in on Travis masturbating to photographs of young boys. It was a bombshell revelation, but an account that would never be proven. Authorities would find no child pornography, or pornography of any kind, on Travis' computer or anywhere in his home.

In the courtroom, Travis' family wept as Jodi kept portraying him as a pervert. Outside court during breaks, friends fumed over her testimony as they gathered in the hallways awaiting her return to the stand.

"She can say whatever she wants, but Travis isn't here to speak for himself," said Julie Haslem, a friend of Travis. "It's bad enough that she took his life. Now she's trying to take his reputation, too."

Her defense attorneys' plan was clear. Build sympathy with jurors. Portray Travis as a cold, emotionless womanizer. Jodi was the victim, Travis the perpetrator.

"What they're doing is trying to elicit sympathy from the jury, to show, look at what this poor person had to go through throughout her life," said California criminal defense lawyer Michael Cardoza.

It's a good technique, he said, but also noted it could backfire if her testimony dragged on too long into the minutia of her life.

"They could start losing some jurors," Cardoza said. "They should really step it up and move it along because if jurors get bored, they could stop paying attention."

And they soon did. Jurors appeared to grow weary of the often-redundant questioning and Jodi's repeated stories, virtually the same thing over and over for days on end.

Now came the details of the killing. Jurors perked up. And the courtroom gallery was packed, not an open seat anywhere.

Jodi explained how she has no recollection of stabbing Travis, slitting his throat or even whether she actually shot him during the fight at his home she described as a battle to save her own life.

Up to this point, Jodi had recalled every single event in her life, dating back decades, in precise detail, right down to specific clothes she wore on a random day, dates, times. But that all changed once she got to the day of Travis' death.

Now, Jodi said, she had a "huge gap" in her memory.

She explained why she lied about her involvement, again noting how she planned to commit suicide and how she didn't want to tarnish Travis' name with lurid details of their sexual relationship, given his public persona as a devout Mormon. She also said she was scared of being arrested, and wanted to keep up the farce to avoid suspicion.

"I just have always heard 'Don't admit to anything,'" she told jurors, explaining she had never been in trouble with the law before and just didn't know how to respond to anyone's questions.

"I knew my life was pretty much over," she told jurors, tears welling up in her eyes.

Spectators whispered to each other in the gallery, wondering whether the tears were for Travis or if Jodi was just petrified at the prospect of being convicted and possibly put to death.

"Do you remember stabbing Travis Alexander?" Nurmi asked.

"I have no memory of stabbing him," Jodi replied. "I remember dropping the knife and it clinked on the tile. . . . And I just remember screaming. I don't remember anything after that."

"I didn't mean to shoot him or anything," she went on to explain. "He was angry at me and he wasn't going to stop. . . . It was like mortal terror."

She said she never called authorities because she was scared.

"I couldn't imagine calling 911 and telling them what I had just done," Jodi said. "I was scared of what would happen to me."

She never once expressed remorse for Travis' death, but instead repeatedly referred to her life being over—either by suicide or arrest.

Her inability to remember key facts of the killing stood in stark contrast to her previous testimony when she recalled the exact type of flavored coffee she ordered at Starbucks in the days leading up to the attack, specific dates of sexual encounters and road trips, and in-depth accounts of stories from 10 years ago.

It was now the prosecutor's turn to cross-examine Jodi, and it would not be cordial. Martinez would unleash a hail of anger on her, trying to trip her up and get her off script after she had two years to rehearse her testimony while incarcerated.

His questioning grew so heated at one point that the judge admonished Jodi and Martinez to stop talking over each other. Jodi mocked Martinez at times, smirking while he stammered in frustration as she alternated between tears and poise, sheepishness and sheer contempt.

"Do you have memory problems, ma'am?" Martinez hounded.

"Sometimes," Jodi replied.

Martinez hammered back, noting it's puzzling that she can't remember such crucial details of the killing, yet "can tell us what kind of coffee you bought at Starbucks sometime back in 2008."

"When do you have memory problems?" Martinez asked, raising his voice. He had set himself up.

"Usually when men like you are screaming at me or grilling me or someone like Travis," Jodi replied calmly, aiming to portray Martinez as the same sort of angry man as Travis working to break her spirit.

The exchange was a high point of drama amid the series of barbs the two traded for days on end.

Martinez would return to the lies, the crux of his case against her. He questioned Jodi about her changing stories, specifically asking about her contention that Travis had broken her finger in a fight before his death.

Martinez reminded Jodi that she told a detective a different story of the broken finger after her arrest.

"Then you testified about it in this court and you gave us another story of how this happened, right?" he said, his voice growing louder with each word.

"No," Jodi said defiantly.

Martinez noted that Jodi made no mention of injuring her finger in a fight with Travis in her journal, where she kept pages of intimate details from her life.

"And no one knew about this supposed or claimed injury to your finger until after you killed Alexander, right?" he said.

"That's right," Jodi replied.

Jurors later watched a video clip of an interview Jodi did with CBS's *48 Hours* in July 2008 while she was in jail.

"Travis' family deserves to know what happened," Jodi said on the show.

Martinez then abruptly stopped the recording.

"They did deserve to know what happened but did they

deserve that lie?" Martinez asked pointedly, noting how at the time of the interview, Jodi was still sticking to the story about the intruders killing Travis.

"I guess not," the ever-evasive Jodi replied.

"Can you imagine how much it must have hurt Mr. Alexander when you stuck that knife into his chest?" Martinez snapped at her loudly.

Defense attorneys immediately objected, and Martinez moved on. He didn't need an answer. He just needed to drive home the point that Travis suffered tremendous pain as she attacked him, a detail he would need to prove to get a shot at a death sentence.

Jodi had now been on the witness stand for 11 days. Her testimony dragged on. And it soon became clear she had been up there too long. She began to slip off script, her quick-witted responses during questioning from her own attorneys shifting to reactive barbs with Martinez. His plan was working. He was wearing her down.

She went from describing in very clinical terms finding Travis "masturbating" to child pornography to using phrases like "jerking off." She no longer referred to him "ejaculating" on her, but instead called it "jizz." For the prosecution, Jodi was showing her true colors. And it played right into their hands.

Martinez noted the conflicting details in Jodi's stories about Travis then and now.

She told authorities, media, friends and family that he was a great person who treated her well. Martinez pointed out text messages she sent Travis just months before she killed him.

"Travis, I thank you for being such an amazing friend. You are a rock, a light and an inspiration," Jodi wrote. "I love you dearly."

Martinez remarked how these messages were sent after Jodi said Travis had been physically abusive on numerous occasions.

"This is not in line with the person you have been talking about, is it?" Martinez prodded.

"Yes, it is very consistent with how he was," Jodi replied.

"You've been telling us before how he was mean?" Martinez said.

"Yes, he also was that," Jodi answered softly, seemingly unsure of how she should respond.

At times, Jodi was holding her own. She became snarky, almost cocky, responding to his yes or no questions by saying, "sure," and "If you say so."

"I'm not having a problem telling the truth," Jodi said at one point.

"But you are having a problem answering my questions, right?" Martinez shot back.

Jodi said the prosecutor's anger was confusing her, making her forget crucial details.

Martinez repeatedly referred to her "litany of lies." He had to keep reminding jurors that Jodi had proven herself to be a liar time and again, and things were no different now that she was on trial for her life.

The prosecutor then went on to his most powerful material—the photos of Travis' bloated, decomposed, and mutilated body. Jodi sobbed uncontrollably, burying her face in her hands.

"Ma'am, were you crying when you were shooting him?" Martinez said.

"I don't remember," Jodi replied, weeping.

"Were you crying when you were stabbing him?" Martinez asked.

"I don't remember," Jodi said softly, her sobs punctuating the silence of the courtroom.

"How about when you cut his throat, were you crying then?" the prosecutor asked, the pitch in his voice reaching an obviously angry tone.

Jodi sobbed as jurors studied her every move.

Martinez continued to press her over the lies, pointing out the absurdity of Jodi leaving Travis a voicemail on his mobile phone within hours of killing him.

Jodi had said earlier that she was trying not to get caught.

"There would be no other reason to leave a dead man a telephone message would there?" Martinez noted.

"Um, that was my goal," Jodi replied.

Martinez later displayed another photograph of Travis' body, his back covered in stab wounds.

"If he's being stabbed in the back, would you acknowledge at that point that he's no threat to you?" Martinez asked.

"I don't know," Jodi responded while still crying, repeating over and over that she just doesn't remember what happened that violent day.

"How could he possibly be a threat to you?" the prosecutor continued.

"I can only guess. I don't know what you're asking me," Jodi responds, obviously flustered.

"All of these lies, ma'am, are meant for your benefit so you can escape responsibility," Martinez noted at one point.

Jodi looked back confused.

"You would have been satisfied to avoid any responsibility for the killing of Mr. Alexander, wouldn't you?" Martinez said.

Jodi paused briefly before replying: "Relieved."

Her testimony at this point began to grow redundant as her

defense attorneys worked to blunt the sting of the prosecutor's ferocious cross-examination.

"Were you forced to testify?" Nurmi asked.

"No," Jodi said.

"When you chose to testify, did you so do with the idea that the lies you told would be called into question?" Nurmi asked.

"Yes," Jodi said, having no problems answering her own attorney's questions.

"Did you go to Mr. Alexander's home on June 4 with the intent on killing him?" Nurmi said.

"No, I didn't," Jodi said. "That was never a thought . . . He was trying to kill me so I was defending myself."

It was now the jury's turn to ask Jodi questions under an uncommon Arizona law that allows panelists to quiz witnesses through written questions read aloud by the judge. The bulk of the queries, about 220 in all, indicated that at least some jurors didn't believe Jodi.

They largely focused on Jodi's contention that she has memory lapses during times of stress and cannot recall crucial details from the day of the killing. They also included queries about why she never tried to help save Travis' life if this was indeed self-defense then repeatedly lied about her involvement.

Many questions were pointed in tone, and seemed to portray a jury struggling to come to grips with Jodi's ever-changing version of events.

"Why were you afraid of the consequences if you killed Travis in self-defense?" one juror asked in a question read by the judge.

"I believed it was not OK . . . to take someone's life even if you were defending yourself," Jodi replied softly, addressing jurors directly with a firm yet gentle gaze.

"Would you decide to tell the truth if you never got arrested?" another juror asked.

Jodi paused briefly, thinking to herself.

"I honestly don't know the answer to that question."

23

THE JURY GETS THE CASE

"This is a manipulative individual who will stop at nothing, and who will continue to be manipulative and will lie at every turn."

—Juan Martinez

It was May 2 as Martinez delivered his dramatic closing arguments. He spent an entire day savaging Jodi as a manipulative liar who will do whatever it takes to save herself and demonize Travis.

He alternated between his trademark boisterous rants and a soft-spoken, cordial approach that hadn't been seen from the hard-nosed prosecutor during the trial. He slammed his hand down on the table for effect then switched to a whisper-like tone. He sounded like a preacher giving a sermon on Sunday morning—powerful pauses interspersed with dramatic inflections and evocative imagery to connect with the jury.

"It's like a field of lies that has sprouted up around her as she sat on the witness stand," Martinez said of Arias' 18 days testifying. "Every time she spat something out, another lie."

Jodi maintained a steely demeanor for the first half of the day, constantly scribbling notes with her pencil, and occasionally gently shaking her head. Then she folded under the heavy emotions brought on by photos from the scene of the killing that Martinez displayed for the jury in the afternoon. She broke down in tears and constantly looked down or away to avoid seeing the images of Travis' mutilated corpse.

There wasn't a dry eye in the front row of the gallery reserved for Travis' family. They sobbed, reached for tissues, and looked on in horror as they relived that terrible June day one last time.

The next day, the defense sought to turn the tables by casting Jodi again as the victim, and Travis as the aggressor. They had plenty of evidence from emails, phone calls, and text messages.

Nurmi began his arguments with the words: "Fear, love, sex, lies, and dirty little secrets." That's what this case is all about, he said. He repeated the phrase several times, underlining for the jury that Travis was nowhere near a saint in his treatment of women, including Jodi.

Nurmi then employed a bold tactic by saying: "It's not about whether or not you like Jodi Arias. Nine days out of ten, I don't like Jodi Arias."

The prosecution objected, prompting Nurmi to move on to another element of the case.

He went on to attack the prosecution's contention that Jodi committed first-degree murder, asking a series of questions aloud to the jury: Why would she rent a car and create such a paper trail if she was indeed engaged in a covert, murderous act? Why would she bother staging a burglary at her grandparents' house if she could have just taken the .25-caliber gun herself? Why would she put a license plate on her car upside down knowing that such an act would be a sure-fire way to get pulled over by police and caught? Why wouldn't she just kill Travis the minute she walked in the door of his house if she indeed was a calculated, cold-blooded killer?

The arguments were crafted with one primary thought in mind: Save Jodi's life, and avoid a first-degree murder conviction.

Nurmi also sought to draw attention away from Jodi's lies: "Nowhere, nowhere in your jury instructions are you asked to convict Jodi Arias of lying."

In the end, nothing about the case against Jodi was completely clear-cut. Jurors heard so many confusing and conflicting stories. The prosecution claimed Jodi fumed with jealousy, yet she told no one anything that would have indicated she felt that way.

Jodi, in turn, claimed Travis was a violent man, had sexual desires for young boys, and owned the very gun she used to kill him. However, just as with the jealousy factor in the prosecution's case, there was no evidence to prove any of Jodi's accusations.

The only account that remained clear throughout—the only point of clarity in the case—was that Jodi killed Travis.

The crux of a conviction came down simply to intent. Was this indeed self-defense as Jodi described? Or a clear case of cold, premeditated murder that deserved no less punishment than what she delivered on Travis—death?

If jurors believed it was premeditated, then Jodi would be guilty of first-degree murder and face either the death penalty or life in prison. If they believed she didn't plan it, but still intentionally caused Travis' death, she would be guilty of second-degree murder and could face a sentence of anywhere from ten to twenty-two years in prison.

If the panel believed she just snapped in the heat of the moment, a crime of passion after "adequate" provocation from

Travis, Jodi would be guilty of manslaughter, and face from seven-to twenty-one years in prison.

And in the extraordinarily rare case that the jury believed everything she said right down to her claim of self-defense, Jodi would be acquitted and walk away a free woman.

On May 3, a hush overtook the courtroom as the judge read the jury the instructions on deliberations. Jodi closed her eyes, clenched her hand in a fist, and covered her face. Travis' family was overwhelmed with emotion, clearly drained after sitting through so much gut-wrenching testimony.

Then, eight men and four women retreated to the jury room one by one as they would struggle to come to grips with the dearth of evidence and Jodi's ever-changing version of events.

After all the tears, after all the lies, after all the stories of steamy sexual escapades, it was time to begin deliberating the fate of Jodi Arias.

Her life was in the jury's hands.

24

THE VERDICT

It took just 15 hours, spread over four days, for the jury to reach a decision.

Media, friends, family, and attorneys got the news that a verdict had been reached in the morning on Wednesday, May 8, 2013. Everyone was directed to return to the courtroom at 1:30 that afternoon.

It had been days of speculation, a weekend of wondering. Guessing what the verdict would be became the most popular parlor game in town. As the previous days passed, reporters gathered outside the courtroom each morning to watch the jurors walk into the deliberation room.

Veteran court reporters always look for clues, studying jurors' hair and makeup, their clothes, anything that would give an indication they had agreed upon a verdict. In many high-profile cases, jurors tend to dress up on verdict day, knowing they will likely be in the spotlight, chased by cameras for interviews.

But there were no clues. The jury dressed as usual. And everyone waited.

Then came Wednesday, and the official announcement from the court. A crowd gathered outside, mostly supporters of Travis praying for the harshest of all penalties.

At about 1:45 p.m., Jodi entered the packed courtroom. As spectators in the gallery rose for the jury, a still silence set in. No one spoke a word.

Cable networks stopped everything they were doing and went to the live feed. Websites froze as the entire world hit the play button to see the next act, the most anticipated event of the entire trial.

Then came the announcement from the female court clerk as she read the verdict form: Count one: First-degree murder. The jury finds the defendant guilty.

Travis' family hugged, cried, and cradled each other—their sighs of relief audible to the entire courtroom. Jodi fought back tears. Willmott gave her a light pat on the back to console her. Reporters rushed to file their stories.

Outside the courthouse, the crowd cheered as if watching their favorite football team score a touchdown. "USA! USA! USA!," they chanted.

The hearing was over almost as quickly as it began. During the next phase of the trial, jurors would determine whether Jodi should qualify for the death penalty.

Family members of Travis and Jodi left the courthouse without speaking to reporters. They would wait until learning her ultimate fate.

But Chris Hughes, a friend of Travis who was supposed to be with him on his trip to Cancun, summed up their feelings for the media gaggle:

"She said, 'No jury would convict me. Mark my words.' This jury convicted her," Hughes said. "Luckily we had twelve smart jurors. They nailed it."

Many of Travis' friends now prayed for the death penalty. Jodi should suffer the same fate as Travis, they said.

An attorney for his family read a statement to the media, explaining that his siblings would soon be filing a wrongful death lawsuit against Jodi, a largely symbolic move given she has no money or assets to take.

And there it was, after more than four months of testimony, the saga of Jodi Arias was finally nearing an end.

But Jodi wasn't done talking. She needed the spotlight at least one more time. She would not go gentle into that good night. That just wasn't her style.

Within minutes of the verdict being read as Jodi sat in a holding cell in the courthouse, she sat down with enterprising TV reporter Troy Hayden of Phoenix Fox affiliate KSAZ, defiant to the end.

Hayden had been working to score this scoop for months, the biggest of his entire career.

It began with a visit to the jail in January for an entirely different story. Hayden used his sources to get to Jodi's cell, and had an initial chat with her through the steel door.

Their relationship grew from there, and Jodi offered him a deal. If she was convicted of first-degree murder, she would give him the interview.

The Sunday before the verdict, Hayden got a voicemail on his office phone. It was from Jodi.

"Hi Troy. It's Jodi Arias. Um, it's Sunday. I just wanted to let you know, um, a deal's a deal," she said. "I'm a person of my word . . . If for some reason the jury comes back with first-degree . . . we can go for it."

It was stunning. She hadn't even been sentenced yet, and could face the death penalty, but she couldn't resist. She sat down before the TV camera once more.

Tears streaming down her cheeks, she explained how she wished she had done things differently, how she wished she had just turned herself into the authorities right after she killed Travis.

"I think if I had just been honest from the beginning, I'd be in a different place," she said in the interview.

She maintained her innocence and pondered aloud how she wished her attorneys had been able to reach a deal with prosecutors long before the trial began.

"My defense team decided to rip the lid off because we were forced to trial," Jodi said. "Um, the state didn't want to settle."

The same jury that convicted her would soon decide whether she should die for her crime or face life in prison.

If the panel decided on life, Jodi would be sent to the Arizona State Prison Complex-Perryville, serving alongside other killers at the maximum-security facility for women on the west side of Phoenix. She would be put to work in the kitchen, on maintenance or janitorial duties, and make anywhere from 10 cents to 50 cents per hour. She would have limited visitation, mostly restricted to weekends.

If she got death, it would still take years for her appeals to play out as she lives under punishing conditions. Death row inmates have little access to the outside world, are confined to their less than 100-square-foot cells for most of the day, and have meals brought to them. They get to shower three times a week.

Jodi's days in the spotlight and the tabloid sensation that enveloped her trial would soon be over like a shooting star fizzling in the darkness.

The TV trucks and media would soon pack up and head to the next courtroom soap opera: a cheating husband somewhere who takes out his wife, a bad mother who kills her kids, a washed-up celebrity whose meltdown comes to a violent end.

This final interview would likely be her last TV appearance for the rest of her life.

And she had a lot to say.

She was asked about Travis' family, but still showed no remorse for her actions, for the brutal killing, for stealing Travis' life.

"I hope that now that a verdict has been rendered, that they're able to find peace, some sense of peace. I don't think they'll ever find the peace that they would like, but maybe they, maybe they'll be able to have greater peace now, or some semblance of it, and be able to move on with their lives and remember their brother the way they want to," Jodi said.

Jodi then pleaded not for forgiveness, not for salvation, not even for life. She wanted freedom.

"I would much rather die sooner than later. Longevity runs in my family, and I don't want to spend the rest of my natural life in one place. You know, I'm pretty healthy. I don't smoke, and I probably would live a long time, so that's not something I'm looking forward to," she said.

"I said years ago that I'd rather get death than life, and that still is true today. I believe death is the ultimate freedom, so I'd rather just have my freedom as soon as I can get it."

ABOUT THE AUTHORS

BRIAN SKOLOFF is an award-winning veteran Associated Press reporter with extensive experience covering some of the nation's most newsworthy stories over the past decade, including the 9/11 terror attacks. He covered the Scott Peterson murder trial, the Fort Hood shootings, and the BP Gulf of Mexico oil spill. Skoloff has covered the Jodi Arias murder trial's nearly every twist and turn, and brings his wealth of experience covering the criminal justice system to this gripping tale of love, lust and death.

JOSH HOFFNER has been a journalist for The Associated Press for 15 years, serving as the lead editor on dozens of major stories all around the country. He worked on the national editing desk at AP headquarters in New York for five years and later served as the city editor for the New York bureau. Hoffner grew up in the Dakotas and graduated from South Dakota State with a journalism degree in 1998.